Buried Alive

A Discussion on Overcoming the "Seven *Lifeless* Sins"

by: J. Jacob Jenkins

PublishAmerica
Baltimore

© 2006 by J. Jacob Jenkins.
All rights reserved. No part of this book may be reproduced, stored in a retrieval system or transmitted in any form or by any means without the prior written permission of the publishers, except by a reviewer who may quote brief passages in a review to be printed in a newspaper, magazine or journal.

First printing

At the specific preference of the author, PublishAmerica allowed this work to remain exactly as the author intended, verbatim, without editorial input.

ISBN: 1-4241-1458-6
PUBLISHED BY PUBLISHAMERICA, LLLP
www.publishamerica.com
Baltimore

Printed in the United States of America

Buried Alive

A Discussion on Overcoming the "Seven *Lifeless* Sins"

Acknowledgments

I recently read about an interview with the Nobel Prize-winning novelist Toni Morrison. In the interview she was asked why she was such a great author. Was it because of certain books she'd read? Was it a particular form or style or approach?

In response Toni Morrison laughed and said, "Oh, no, that is not why I am a great writer. I am a great writer because when I was a little girl and walked into a room where my father was sitting, his eyes would light up. That is why I am a great writer. That is why. There isn't any other reason."[1]

I know that I will never be a Nobel Prize-winning novelist. And I know that I will never be as great of a writer as Toni Morrison is. Yet I still relate to her response.

If you were to ask me where I found the inspiration to write this book I would claim no credit for myself. And if you find a single word of encouragement within its pages, or a single insight, I claim no responsibility. Instead, I give full recognition to those who have loved me throughout the years; those who have sustained and encouraged me unconditionally. I point to my fiancée and my family and my friends.

"That is why," I say, "There isn't any other reason."

✝

Because of this I would like to thank my fiancée Brecca. —A woman whose love and beauty and sincerity are rivaled only by her humility.

I would like to thank my entire family, especially mom and dad, Josh and Jennifer. —You epitomize the words of support and stability.

I would like thank my closest friends, especially Buckle, Pollack, Nick, Russ, Lyons, and the list goes on. —It's been fun.

Lastly, and obviously, I would like to thank God. —All of language is inadequate.

Thank you all.
I couldn't have written a single word without you.

Contents

Author's Note	11
Introduction	13
The Safari of Life	14
An Entirely Different Sort of List	16
Not Evil, Just Lifeless	17
Chapter 1: Tolerance	21
Congenial Christianity	24
The Beauty of Belief	25
Our Itching Ears *or* The Truth of a Triple Bypass	28
Good News for All People	30
Chinese Goose Berries *or* The Enemy of Sincere Love	31
Critiquing Paul	33
Time to Take a Stand	34
Chapter 2: Fundamentalism	39
To Dance with the Divine	41
The Greatest Fundamental	44
In Light of Love	46
Love as an End	48
Trivial Theologies *or* Old Highway 91	49
The Reality of Relativity	51
The Eternal Canvas	54
Unfinished Christians	56
Live to Love, Dare to Dance	58
Afterthought: Recommended Readings for Fundamentalism	60
Chapter 3: Compromise	61
Ranting about Armageddon	64
The Real Problem	65

Being the Solution	66
Casualties of Compromise	67
[Insert Your Name Here]	69
See God for More Details	70
Step One: Not Proud	74
Step Two: The Lure of Christ	76
An Understanding *or* How to Properly Operate a Blender	78
Day Old Meatloaf	79

Chapter 4: Materialism   *81*

Ensnared by the Finite	84
Twisted Values (a.k.a. American Values)	85
The Reality of Our Actions *or* If Kalinga Were Your Son	88
A Street Corner Named Desire *or* What We are Worth	89
Our Own Stupid Pocketbook	92
The Divine Paradox	94
Grasping the Infinite	96
Learning to Let Go	99
Afterthought: Ways to Let Go	101

Chapter 5: Busyness   *103*

Someone Like Trevor	107
A Loss of Direction	108
Plotting a Course	109
What You Can Chew	111
To Enjoy Life	115
Number 34	117
Things that Matter, Things that Last	118
Afterthought: 33 *More* Ways to Enjoy Life	121

Chapter 6: Laziness   *123*

Faith, Grace & A Little Work *or* A Prayer of Procrastination	127
Opening Car Doors *or* Love Made Visible	129
Some Sort of Miraculous Bank Account	133
What We've Been Entrusted	135
Ridiculous Laziness	138
More than a Worn Out Cliché	140

Chapter 7: Comfort   *143*

    The Most Important Chapter of this Entire Book   146
    Scripture You Won't Likely Hear Preached on this Sunday
    at Church   147
    God & Logic   149
    The Third Option: Embracing Scripture, Embracing God   152
    Your Spouse is Not an Encyclopedia (And Neither is God)   153
    The Worship of Wonder   158
    A God Too Great   160

Epilogue   *165*

    The Choice is Yours *or* Our Cardboard Worlds   166

Questions for Further Discussion   *169*

Endnotes   *177*

Author's Note

I will never be worthy to write a book.
Yet as it turns out that may be my greatest qualification for writing this one.

You see, I have spent the majority of my life by living lifelessly. Most days I still manage to squander an hour or two or three or…
If anyone were keeping score I'm sure I'd have my doctorate in lifelessness by now. Like some sort of connoisseur I'd lounge poolside with a big cigar tucked between my back teeth and dispense professional advice at an hourly rate on how you too could be lifeless.
That's because I am guilty of every sin in the pages to come. And any bit of wisdom you gleam from them has been learned by me in the hardest of ways.
So as you can tell, I may be young and I'm certainly foolish. But I know what it means to be human. I know how it feels to be unfinished, incomplete, desperate and needy. Inside and out I know what it's like to be lifeless.
And *that* is my greatest qualification of all.

No doubt about it, I will never be worthy to write a book.
So, I write…

Introduction

"Now choose life, so that you and your children may live...for the Lord is your life."[2]

—Moses

"You broke the bonds and you
Loosed the chains
Carried the cross
Of my shame
Of my shame
You know I believed it
But I still haven't found what I'm looking for."
—U2,"I Still Haven't Found What I'm Looking For"

"I do not think the devil cares how many churches you build, if only you have lukewarm preachers and people in them."

—C. H. Spurgeon

    It stood only a few feet away from me with nothing but air between us.

    It stomped at the ground, sending bellows of dust into the sky. It lifted its massive head, sending out a trumpet call. It reared its body to charge, sending chills down my spine.

    I sat motionless, truly petrified. My eyes were bright with wonder and wide with terror. My heart was pounding noisily in my chest. My mind churned.

    I had seen an endless number of elephants before. I'd seen them on television. I'd seen them in movies and books and magazines. But none of those times could have prepared me for this one. Seeing an elephant on television can never compare to when the glass screen between it and you is removed. Seeing a fourteen inch photograph can never measure up to a fourteen foot reality.

That is the difference between watching "Animal Planet" at home in your Lay-Z—Boy and experiencing a safari in the African bush.

Similarly, it is the difference between the life many of us are living and the life we were intended to live.

The Safari of Life

In time the elephant backed down. It slowly turned and strolled away as if the air were as thick as water. As it did I exhaled a suspended sigh. And smiled. I had never felt so alive.

Over the years I have held tightly to that memory. I never want to let it go. For me it is a constant reminder of what so many people fail to ever realize.

You see, many people have no idea what they are missing. Christ has offered each of us a life unlike anything we have ever known or could ever imagine; a life that breaks all the rules of this world; a radical journey of wonder and pleasure that begins today and reaches into eternity. Yet many of us never realize that we're meant for more. As Christians we never seem to consider that the life we're living is a mere glimpse of what it could be.

"I have come that you may have life, and have it to the full."[3]

"The Spirit gives life."[4]

"…So that His life may be revealed in our mortal body."[5]

"In Him was life, and that life was the light of men."[6]

"God made you alive with Christ."[7]

"Godliness has value for all things, holding promise for both the present life and the life to come."[8]

"But small is the gate and narrow is the road that leads to life, and only a few find it."[9]

BURIED ALIVE: A DISCUSSION ON OVERCOMING THE "SEVEN LIFELESS SINS"

"The life appeared; we have seen it and testify to it."[10]

As children we seemed to have known that there is more to this existence of ours. We voyaged and we explored. We sung and we danced. The skies were the limit, and even they couldn't damper our imaginations.

Yet so many years have now gone by that we've forgotten. Or else we've given up. So many years have passed since our souls savored true adventure that we've all but abandoned the hope of ever tasting it again.

As a result, many of our lives are like the fairgrounds a day after the carnival has left town. You can almost hear the laughter of children playing. You can almost see the rides and games and crowds of people. You can almost smell the hotdogs and taste the funnel cakes.

But not quite.

Instead you hear only silence. You see an empty field with used napkins and torn ticket stubs blowing past like tumbleweed. You smell the remnants of a day gone by, and you taste the eerie absence of something missing.

Life as a safari? More like life as bland survival. We aren't sure where we went wrong but we know that something isn't right.

We once dreamed of changing this world. Now we're stuck in a dead end job. We once had hopes and goals and aspirations. Now, more than anything else, we look forward to watching television.

Somehow, somewhere along the way, our hearts have been hardened and our dreams have been dulled. We've traded ambition for obligation and passion for duty. We've forsaking the cries of our heart for the expectations of society. In fact, when you cut through the façade many of us are like Mike…

"On September 10, 1945 a Wyandotte chicken named Mike had its head chopped off but went on to survive for 18 months. Mike's owner, Lloyd Olsen, fed and watered the headless chicken directly into his gullet with an eyedropper. Mike eventually choked to death on a corn kernel in an Arizona motel."[11]

We are living, but is this what it means to be alive? We may be alive, but is this all there is to life? Is this what Christ meant when He offered us life to the full, or is there *more*?

An Entirely Different Sort of List

The hippopotamus is one of my favorite animals. It's so big and clumsy looking, so fat and gray and ugly. Honestly, when I look at one I sometimes wonder what God was thinking. I love His creativity.

I say all of this to make a point. When you and I consider deadly, dangerous animals we probably think of lions and tigers, snakes and sharks. I doubt any of us think of hippopotamuses. But at it turns out, they are more deadly than most people realize.

Lurking just below the waters' murky surface, hippos can go completely unnoticed. Even when they are spotted their presence is often overlooked. But if their territory is threatened the hippopotamus can strike in an instant. They can carve an entire vessel in half with their enormous mouth and teeth, leaving behind a fatal wake of death and destruction. For this reason many experts believe hippopotamuses kill more people each year than any other animal, making them the most dangerous creature in the world.

When I consider my life, the struggle I have of living it to the full and what it is that keeps me from doing so, I am often reminded of the clumsy, ugly hippo. That's because the most harmful and dangerous of sins are not always the most obvious. Rather, they are the most subtle and elusive. And they are not what we would usually expect, but rather what we would least imagine.

†

Pope St. Gregory the Great, who reigned from 590-604, distinguished these as the seven capital sins: pride, envy, wrath, sloth, greed, gluttony, and lust. They have since become known as the "seven deadly sins." Sermons have been preached on them. Movies have been made about them. Endless books have been written in regard to them.

This is *not* one of those books.

As utterly detrimental as these sins are, I believe there's an entirely different sort of list that needs to be made. As tight a grasp as these sins have on our world today there's another list that has gone entirely unnoticed. Like the ugly hippo, it has remained below the radar and just out of view. It has been overlooked and even dismissed, and in doing so it has subtly polluted our society for years. The list I am speaking of is:

BURIED ALIVE: A DISCUSSION ON OVERCOMING THE "SEVEN LIFELESS SINS"

Tolerance
Fundamentalism
Compromise
Materialism
Busyness
Laziness
Comfort.

This list of the "seven *lifeless* sins" may not rob you of your eternal life, but it will suffocate your present one. It may not keep you from entering the eternal presence of God, but it will keep you from the safari of life. Like a living purgatory it will render you lifeless.

For as Christians the enemy cannot kill us. So he aspires instead to bury us alive.

Not Evil, Just Lifeless

He had made the trek from Jerusalem to Jericho more times than he could remember. As a child he would hike the rocky, desert path bartering goods to support his family. As an adult, little had changed.

He walked along, offering his usual wares to his usual customers: Fifty shekels of salt for Dr. David…A piece of pottery for the widow of Gilgal…Four cubits of wool for the young Malachi, who reminded him so much of his own son.

The day was going well. It was not unlike any other. But in an instant all of that changed.

There was a sudden rush of sound behind him. Then there was a swift pain to the back of his head. Then there was nothing but blackness.

It all happened so quickly that he never saw it coming. Two men had struck him from behind. They had beaten him again and again, robbed him, and then left him along the edge of the road. Helpless. Dying. Alone.

The man drifted in and out of consciousness. He knew that he was dying, and he knew that he may never see his son again. Yet there seemed to be nothing he could do about it.

Then suddenly he heard a faint sound of footsteps walking along the path. The sound grew closer and closer until it was right along side him. Barely able to muster enough strength, the man opened one eye. He was unable to clearly focus but he could discern that the passing traveler was a priest. The man closed his eye and sighed a smile at his own good fortune. Surely a priest would help him in whatever way he could.

But the footsteps continued on.

The priest had seen the fallen man lying helplessly along the road. But rather than help he had looked the other way. Rather than stopping he had passed by on the other side.

The day wore on. The sun fell low on the horizon. The man knew that if he was not helped before nightfall he would not survive until dawn.

Then suddenly he heard another set of footsteps. They too grew closer and closer until they were right along side him. But they too never stopped.

This time the traveler was a Levite. He had also saw the man bleeding, naked along the edge of the road. But rather than help he too had looked the other way. Rather than stopping he too had passed by on the other side.

As the second set of footsteps moved further away, so did the man's hopes of ever seeing his family again. The sun retreated behind Mount Nebo. The man slipped again into a deep unconsciousness. The last thing he heard was a third set of footsteps approaching. But he didn't bother to look again. He didn't bother to hope.

Yet this time the footsteps came to a halt. There was the sound of sandals shuffling in the sand as the third traveler leaned over him. There was the sound of a colt in the distance. Then there was the sound of shredding cloth.

The third traveler had begun to tear his own robe, making crude bandages for the wounded man. (Luke 10: 25-37)

✝

The parable of the good Samaritan is a familiar story to many of us. But don't let familiarity cause you to overlook a vital truth.

Notice the way Jesus works to contrast the first two men who passed by to the third man who stopped to offer help. He contrasts the ruthlessness of the first two men to the kindness of the third. He contrasts

*BURIED ALIVE: A DISCUSSION ON OVERCOMING THE
"SEVEN LIFELESS SINS"*

the heartlessness of the priest and Levite to the love of the Samaritan.

But sometimes I wonder, *what about the robbers?!* After all, the priest and the Levite didn't beat the man or leave him for dead. All they did is pass him by on the other side of the road.

And that is precisely the point.

They didn't harm the stranger, but they didn't help him either. They didn't necessarily do anything wrong, but they failed to do what was truly right. They weren't evil, just lifeless.—And I imagine most of us can relate.

You see, it is not usually the sins of murder and death that paralyze us as Christians. We don't ordinarily have twelve mistresses. We don't typically drink or gamble our lives away. We don't frequently rob travelers and leave them for dead.

Rather, we just pass by on the other side.

We so *tolerate* the beliefs of this world that we lose sight of our own. We become so wrapped in the *fundamental* teachings of our Christian religion that we overlook their point. We *compromise* with the world for so long that we cease to be its salt. We so blindly accept American *materialism* that we fail to ever see it as the vice that it is. We live such *busy* lives that we forget the things that matter most. We embrace a level of *laziness* that keeps from living our lives to the full. And lastly, we become so *comfortable* in our spiritual walks that we never challenge or change any of this.

That is what it means to be buried alive. It's not that we are wicked, evil people. We are not deadly sinners. But as we've discussed here, the issue is not so much about wickedness and death as it is about apathy and lifelessness.

We may not be criminals, but are we passionately pursuing a life of good?

We may have gone to church on Sunday, but did our lives reflect it Monday through Saturday?

Perhaps we haven't been horrible spouses or parents this week, but have we been the most loving we can be?

We aren't dead yet, but are we truly alive?

Those are the questions we must ask ourselves. Those are the standards we must set for ourselves. And that is what this book is about.

It's about raising our current standard of living from lifeless to *"the life that is truly life.*"[12] It's about moving beyond mundane mediocrity to something genuine, fresh and real. It's about pushing past bland survival so that you and I can take hold of something passionate and purposeful and inspiring.

For as it turns out, the greatest battle most Christians face is not one of good and evil, but rather one of good and lifelessness.

†

So, if you are a vile and wicked person then this book is probably not meant for you.

And if you are some sort of saint, living each and every day to the full, bursting with love and passion and truth, then this book is certainly not meant for you.

But if you're anything like me, just an average Christian somewhere in between, trying to do your best in this world we live, then turn the page.

A safari awaits…

Chapter 1

Tolerance

Tolerance

"For now we really live, since you are standing firm in the Lord."[13]
—the Apostle Paul

"May you always know the truth
And see the lights surrounding you.
May you always be courageous,
Stand upright and be strong,
—Bob Dylan, "Forever Young"

"Truth becomes hard if it is not softened by love; love becomes soft if it is not strengthened by truth."
—John Stott

Last night I dreamed that I died.

I watched my own funeral service as if I were a fly on the wall. I watched as people clad in black silently filled the room, greeting my family and offering their last respects. It was a solemn and peaceful service, with distant relatives and old, forgotten friends. It was a big turn out, and that was good to see. As far as watching ones own funeral goes I suppose it was as pleasant as you could expect.

But then suddenly my dream turned into a nightmare.

As the guests took their seats a minister stood to deliver my eulogy. He walked to the podium and cleared his throat and glanced around at the many faces. He forced a gentle smile and then he began: "Jacob was a nice man." I gasped. If flies could speak I would have called out in protest. But I couldn't. So I didn't. And he continued, "Jacob was always nice to everyone he met. He lived a nice life…"

I woke up in a cold sweat.

Congenial Christianity

No, I didn't really have that dream last night. But such a reality is my nightmare.

I don't want to live a "nice" life. I certainly don't want to be remembered as having been merely "nice." Instead I want my life to be passionate and inspiring. I want to be an adventurer and a lover. I want to be courageous, bold, daring, and maybe even a little dangerous.

But not nice.

Never just nice.

I say all of this because it seems many Christians today have set niceness up on a pedestal as if it were the ultimate goal of their lives. As if the great commission instructed us, "Therefore go and be nice to all nations," many of us have come to value politeness and courtesy above all else. We have come to seek open-mindedness and approval at all cost.

We do not want to offend anyone, so we tolerate. We do not want to disagree with anyone, so we tolerate. And we, heaven forbid, do not want to bring up the name or issue of Jesus Christ, so we tolerate.

We had rather swallow lies than stand strong for the truth. We had rather permit deceit than appear ugly or small-minded. As a result, the movement described in Acts as having *"caused trouble all over the world"*[14] has since been sacrificed at the alter of congeniality.

In the end, Christianity for many of us has become about as bland as a school lunch, so afraid of offending someone that it fails to satisfy anyone. It doesn't inspire. It no longer stirs. It doesn't even attempt to challenge, provoke or stimulate. Instead, it is nice.

And mere niceness is lifeless.

†

Of course I'm not advocating bigotry, prejudice or narrow-mindedness. In truth, narrow-mindedness should not be the point any more than niceness should be the point.

So although this chapter is a discussion on the dangers of tolerance I believe a library of books could, and should, be written on the need for it. In fact I hope to turn our attention that way in the very next chapter. For I believe this world can never have too much love and acceptance. Both love and acceptance were at the heart of Christ's teachings.

Yet, having said that, I believe the type and level of tolerance that currently ravages our nation has little to do with the teachings of Christ. Rather, it has served to overthrow these very foundations of biblical principle. It has corroded our moral compass, and has left us adrift in a sea of relativity. In the end it has taken us further from the teachings of Christ rather than nearer, and it has left us less capable of love rather than more.

As a result, many Christians today are living out a flimsy and fickle faith. They are more concerned with pleasing others than with seeking truth; more concerned with being nice than standing strong. They seem to have forgotten their own values and have come to overlook the beauty of belief.

The Beauty of Belief

Some years ago a young woman arrived at our Bible study in tears. Her husband had visited his doctor earlier that morning for a routine check up. During his visit the doctor had found a blemish on the lining of his stomach.

It was cancer.

This young woman was not naïve to the threat. Cancer had already reared its ugly head in her life several times before. It had already taken several of those closest to her.

It was a warm summer evening, but her body was shivering from a bitter chill. And so one by one we began to gather around her in loving support. We offered her kind words of condolence. We shared in her sorrow, her tears. Then we prayed.

We prayed for her husband's health. We prayed for his future. We put his life in God's hands, frankly praying for a miracle.

I will never forget opening my eyes after some time of prayer and looking around at the other faces in our group. I remember looking at their sincere, fervent expressions and —if I may be so honest—*I thought it all seemed a bit ridiculous.*

I mean, it was nice what we were doing. We were being supportive as a church family, and we were showing this young woman how much we cared. But did we really expect God to physically heal her husband?

I called myself a Christian at the time and I said I believed in God. I even spoke of His influence in my own life. But I couldn't help to wonder, in today's modern day and age should we really expect God to move in such a powerful way?

It's probably a good thing I wasn't the only person praying, because during their next doctor's visit the surgeons found *no sign of cancer!*

They said there must have been some kind of mistake. They apologized, and attributed it to human error. They explained it away. But they could never explain it.

Just as clearly as that night we prayed for a miracle I remember the morning she shared her story with the rest of our church family. Amidst everyone else's excitement of experiencing God first hand and the joy of being a part of His plan, I hung my head in shame. I had been a professed Christian for years, but that morning I realized I had only been dabbling in half-belief. I had been living lifelessly.

Jesus is the only way?[15] Of course. But then again, there are many different paths to God, right?

The Bible is God's holy word?[16] Certainly. Except maybe for that part about creation[17]....and that part about adultery[18]....and abortion[19]...and...

God performs miracles?[20] Absolutely. But we don't actually expect Him to, do we?

I realized that morning that I had been masquerading through my Christian life. In truth I had no idea what I really believed, and I often disagreed with *myself.* So that morning I made the decision to finally make a decision. I decided, then and there, what I truly believed.

Of course there were still question marks left to be settled, but at least I knew now where they were. There was a lot of growth yet to be accomplished, but at least I'd taken the first step.

Now, all I had to do was take another.

And then another.

†

In our pursuit of tolerance it seems that many of us have lost our foundation and understanding of Biblical truth. We have allowed the beliefs of this world to infiltrate the folds of God's church. In the end, we've created some kind of hybrid, half-truth, contradicting religion.

It says Jesus is the Savior. But then it accepts that there are other avenues to God.

It says the Bible is truth. But then it disagrees with most of it.

It says God. But then it treats Him like a god.

Tolerance has led to uncertainty. Uncertainty has led to confusion. Confusion has led to misunderstanding. As a result, *many Christians no longer know what it even means to be a Christian.* Consider these facts and see for yourself:

- More than half of America (56%) say that "if a person is generally good, or does enough good things for others during their life, they will earn a place in heaven."[21]

- Of those who have made a personal commitment to Jesus Christ, 40 percent do *not* believe that their commitment alone will get them to Heaven.[22]

- A recent survey found that 88% of Americans are certain they are going to heaven. Yet the very same survey showed that only 67% of Americans are certain there even is a heaven.[23]

- 10 percent of self-identified Protestants and 21 percent of Catholics do not even believe in *God*.[24]

Gallup says that such a high degree of religious tolerance reflects, in part, "not only a lack of knowledge of other religions but an ignorance of one's own faith." In some polls, he says, "You have Christians saying, 'Yes, Jesus is the only way.' And also saying, 'Yes, there are many paths to God.' It's not that Americans don't believe anything; they believe everything."[25]

Perhaps the reason Christianity no longer stands strong in America is because its members no longer know where to stand. Like me on that Sunday morning years ago, perhaps we all need to finally decide what it is that we believe.

†

So, what do *you* believe?

The question is not what your friends and family believe, what your church believes, or even what you say you believe. It is directed at you, and what beliefs you're willing to stand on and stand for. I challenge you to take a moment and honestly consider this question. Then take a moment of honesty to record your answer at the end of this chapter.

By asking this I'm not trying to push your beliefs in any particular direction. I hope only to push them in some direction. And I'm certainly not trying to mold your values into mine. Rather, I hope only to help you realize your own.

Scripture says, "*I know your deeds, that you are neither cold nor hot. I wish you were either one or the other!*"[26] For that reason we can no longer afford to stand on the fence. Or even worse, to stand on both sides.

Choose death, or choose life.—The choice is yours. But please, no more lifelessness. No more lip service. No more mixed words and half-belief. For whatever you and I believe to be true, we must start living it.

This is all under the assumption, of course, that there is such a thing as truth…

Our Itching Ears or The Truth of a Triple Bypass

Once upon a time there was a thing called truth. However, many Americans today believe themselves to be wiser than those of decades past. They believe any attempt to define morality was only a human endeavor of ancient history. They believe truth can only be defined on an individual basis, by and for each individual person.

As a result, these people have moved beyond such barbaric ideals as objective truth and morality. They have overcome such uncivilized thinking. They have since become "enlightened."

Yet this enlightened idea of relative truth is actually nothing new. The Old Testament book of Judges tells of a time when relativism reigned: "*In those days Israel had no king; everyone did as he saw fit.*"[27] And a few hundred years later, when Jesus was faced with crucifixion, Pilate asked Him, "*What is truth?*"[28]

In reality Pilate's question is a hard one to answer. The quest demands our whole self. And the answer we find is never quite the answer we were searching for.

Relative truth on the other hand is easy. It's as simple as what we already believe, and it always suits our lifestyle of choice.

> "*For the time will come when men will not put up with sound doctrine. Instead, to suit their own desires, they will gather around them a great number of teachers to say what their itching ears want to hear.*"[29]

Truth by definition is exclusive. But it seems that our itching ears have embraced their own reality. In the process truth has all but died and has been replaced by our own personal opinions.

For that reason the word "true" now means nothing more than "true for me." And the words "right" and "wrong" are meaningless.

However, if truth and morality are really relative then that means there is no moral distinction between the actions of Mother Teresa and Adolf Hitler. If truth and morality are really relative then that means there is nothing wrong with rape or incest or with torturing infants, because there is no so such thing as *wrong*.

In the end, it seems that proponents of relativity support it in just the right degree so that their own opinion is accurate and anyone who disagrees with them is not.

†

Don't misunderstand me, there is some legitimacy to relativity. Degrees of relativity are as biblical as the absolute truth of Jesus Christ.[30] (More on reconciling these views in the next chapter.) Yet again, our problem lies within the style and degree of relativity that has emerged in much of America today.

We have moved beyond truth which allows room for relativity.

We currently have relativity which allows no room for truth.

†

When you toss congenial Christians into this emerging climate of relativity it is easy to see how we've become so confused. Without a foundation of Biblical understanding it is easy to see how we've become so overly tolerant. After all, if you stand for nothing then you'll fall for anything.

But the simple fact is that all religions cannot be correct when they all disagree with one another. All religions simply cannot point to the same God when they are all pointing in different directions. Ravi Zacharias comments on this by writing, "At the heart of *every* religion is an uncompromising commitment to a particular way of defining who God is or is not and accordingly...Every religion at its core is exclusive."[31]

In truth, a committed Muslim cannot possibly believe that an Orthodox Jew's faith is real. A committed Mormon simply cannot accept the beliefs of Hinduism. As Zacharias said, every religion at its core is exclusive.

And Christianity is no exception:

"For there is one God and one mediator between God and men, the man Christ Jesus, who gave himself as a ransom for all men."[32]

"He who has the Son has life; he who does not have the Son of God does not have life."[33]

"Jesus answered, 'I am the way and the truth and the life. No one comes to the Father except through me.'"[34]

"Salvation is found in no one else, for there is no other name under heaven given to men by which we must be saved."[35]

"No one knows the Son except the Father. Nor does anyone know the Father except the Son, and the one to whom the Son wills to reveal Him."[36]

"There shall be one flock and one shepherd."[37]

I am continually dismayed by the level of spiritual tolerance that Christianity has come to accept as normal. In no other facet of life would such a tolerant mindset be accepted. No matter how much we valued 'niceness', we would never stand idly by and allow a doctor to decide where *she* believes our heart is, how *she* believes it works, and how *she* believes a triple bypass should be done. A doctor would know better. A patient would expect better.

We demand more when it comes to our body. Why then do we settle for less when it comes to our soul?

Good News for All People

Having said all of this, I wish to make one thing very clear: *Jesus Christ is not an obstacle to salvation.*

The other night I was watching Larry King Live with my fiancée Brecca. There were several prominent Christian leaders on the show and so we were really enjoying things when suddenly Brecca realized something.

These Christian leaders were clearly using this opportunity to spread the news of Christ, and though that was good, Brecca recognized that their words sounded more like words of rejection than words of acceptance. She pointed out that what they had to say sounded more like *bad* news than it did *"good news of great joy...for all the people"*[38]

That's because in combating the current climate of relativity we as Christians often overstate the exclusiveness of Christ. We get so caught up in proving our point that we miss the point. We get so caught up in making our case that we make Christ out to be some sort of elitist bigot.

So, in quoting John 14:6 we often speed through Christ's words, *"I am the way and the truth and the life."* Then we overstate, *"No one comes to the Father except through me."* As a result, Jesus is seen as a barrier rather than as a bridge. And He is used as an opportunity to write off unbelievers rather than an opportunity to embrace them.

But the point is not that Jesus is the only way, as if He is a blockade between man and God. The point is that through Christ there is a way. Jesus in fact overcomes the blockade! *"For God did not send His Son into the world to condemn the world, but to save the world through Him."*[39]

For this reason you and I mustn't slam the door shut on those who do not believe in Christ. Rather, we must offer them sincere love, and accept them unconditionally. Only then, as Brecca would say, may we show them the one true door standing wide open.

Chinese Goose Berries or The Enemy of Sincere Love

Pineapples, mangos, tangerines, Chinese goose berries.... Chinese goose what? For some reason that name just isn't too appetizing. Perhaps that is why the Chinese goose berry has become better known in America as *kiwi*.

From tropical fruits to lifeless sins we all realize the amazing difference a label can make. And so, we have become rather skilled at justifying our actions by labeling them differently.

We silently work along side a coworker who indulges one affair after another, and we say we are being "accepting." We remain quiet when a friend decides to abort an unwanted baby, and we say we are being "understanding." We live day after day and year after year silently keeping the good news of Christ to ourselves, and we say we are being "considerate."

But whatever we call it, it is not what we have been called to do. Whatever we label it, it is still a goose berry.

Scripture says, *"faithful are the wounds of a friend, but deceitful are the kisses of an enemy."*[40] Such tolerance is the kiss of an enemy. It is less concerned with being accepting as it is with being accepted. It is less concerned with being understanding as it is with being misunderstood. It is less concerned with being considerate as it is with simply being liked.

Seventy percent of Christians in America say that Christianity should be tolerant of other faiths and simply leave them alone.[41] But if we as Christians believe what we say we believe; if Jesus Christ is our Lord; if He has made a genuine impact on our lives and accomplished in us a *new creation*[42], then how can we possibly remain silent as friends and family live their entire lives without knowing Him?

In fact, an Arab proverb asks: "What is the greatest crime in the world? It is finding water and remaining silent." That is what it's like when we as Christians keep a 'silent witness'. It is not love. It is a *crime*.

Jesus loved the people of this world more than you and I could ever imagine. So when He began His ministry He didn't proclaim, "Hey, don't worry about anything. Just keep living the way you are and keep believing the way you do." Rather, the first words of Christ's ministry were, *"Repent, for the kingdom of heaven is near."*[43] Because of His love, not despite it, Jesus spoke convicting and even disturbing words. Because He loved the people of this world Jesus proclaimed the *truth*.

So, as it turns out 'niceness' is the enemy of sincere love. If we truly loved—if we truly cared about other people more than our own stupid likeability—we would not tolerate in the way that we so often do. We would not stand idly by, coveting the truth of Christ in our hearts.

As Christians such tolerance cannot possibly be love. Rather, when we tolerate in such a way we love only ourselves.

†

My friend Danny would argue that if we loved our neighbors we'd tolerate their diverse lifestyles. After all, aren't we all sinners? And weren't we all uniquely designed by our Maker?

I think Danny is on to something. There is a lot of truth in his reasoning about the way we should accept and forgive others; loving them as we love ourselves. However, I disagree with my friend when it comes to denying the realities of sin in order to do so.

After all, for you to love your spouse or son or daughter do you first convince yourself that he or she is flawless? Of course not. If you did you would only be kidding yourself. In the same way, true love rises above the realities of our human nature. It does not merely gloss over or deny them.

So, you and I must love all peoples no matter how uniquely diverse they are from us. We must cultivate an appreciation for individuality. We must learn to savor the art of our Master's hand. But we needn't sacrifice scriptural truth or deny the realities of sin in order to do so.

For in the end we must learn to love in truth before we can ever truly love.

Critiquing Paul

Recently I read a USA Today poll that asked parents to grade their involvement in their kid's education. The poll found that over 8 in 10 parents gave themselves high marks (A's and B's). However, when these same parents were asked to assess the involvement of other parents nearly 8 in 10 gave C's, D's and even F's.[44]

The Bible clearly says, *"let us stop passing judgment on one another,"*[45] and this survey shows precisely why: We simply aren't any good at it! We are just too good at seeing the faults of others, while ignoring and denying and excusing our own.

However, having said that, in today's climate of congenial Christianity and moral relativism the idea of judging has been largely overstated and has often been taken completely out of its context. As a result, Christians are often so scared of appearing judgmental that they're afraid to seek truth, and they're so worried of being labeled a bigot that they're not discerning.

Jesus spoke bluntly on this issue, saying, *"When you see a cloud rising in the west, immediately you say, 'It's going to rain,' and it does. And when the south wind blows, you say, 'It's going to be hot,' and it is. Hypocrites! You know how to interpret the appearance of the earth and the sky. How is it that you don't know how to interpret this present time? Why don't you judge for yourselves what is right?"*[46]

†

It seems that many Christians today are so uncertain of their own beliefs that they're afraid to judge for themselves what is right. Yet throughout Scripture believers are praised for their diligent discernment. In fact, the book of Acts tells us of a church in Berea that *"examined the Scriptures every day to see if what Paul said was true."*[47] With a solid foundation of Biblical understanding they actually critiqued the great apostle Paul. With a clear understanding of scripture they discerned for themselves whether his words were true.

So, were the Bereans being critical of Paul? Were they judging his alleged claims? Of course! They were responding exactly as wise believers should.

"The wise in heart are called discerning."[48]

"Test everything. Hold on to the good. Avoid every kind of evil."[49]

"Dear friends, do not believe every spirit, but test the spirits to see whether they are from God, because many false prophets have gone out into the world. This is how you can recognize the Spirit of God: Every spirit that acknowledges that Jesus Christ has come in the flesh is from God, but every spirit that does not acknowledge Jesus is not from God."[50]

You see, we must never judge the spiritual condition of some one else because we can never see their true heart or know their true intentions. Instead, Christ has called us to love. He has instructed us to offer acceptance. He has commanded us to forgive.

However, when someone proclaims that Muhammad, Buddha, Mary Baker Eddy, Joseph Smith, Gandhi, or Mother Mary is the true path to God, it is our *responsibility* to be discerning. As it turns out, such an instance requires no judgment at all. It requires only the faith and understanding of what we say we believe. It requires only that we stand up and stand strong for what we hold to be true.

Time to Take a Stand

Isaac the Bruce is the true heir to the Scottish throne. But he is not a true leader. He struggles between the expectations of others and his own aspirations. He wrestles between obligation and desire; apprehension and ambition. William Wallace on the other hand knows nothing other than a life of courageous leadership.

Wallace stands face to face with the pristine Bruce, himself clad in leather, fur, dust, and muck. He looks deep into Bruce's eyes. Searching. Then he speaks, continuing to search with each spoken word, "Your title gives you claim to the throne of our country, but

BURIED ALIVE: A DISCUSSION ON OVERCOMING THE "SEVEN LIFELESS SINS"

men don't follow titles, they follow courage...and *if you would just lead them* to freedom they'd follow you.—And so would I."

†

I love the movie *Braveheart*. I think all guys do. Deep in our hearts I think we all want to be impassioned and courageous like Mel Gibson's character was. For that reason this obscure scene from the epic film never ceases to stir me. It is as if my own heart is the one being searched. It is as if the words are pulling at my soul.

...if you would just lead them...

In the same way I believe that God is tugging at the soul of American Christianity. He has seen the starving masses, for *"the harvest is plentiful but the workers are few."*[51] He has placed each of us exactly where He desires us to be, *"for such a time as this."*[52] And now He is searching our hearts, pulling at our souls, saying, *"If you would just lead them* then they would come to know Me."

Have you ever wondered why the simple truth of Christ alludes so many, while the heresies of this world enslave so many? Have you ever wondered how millions of people have acquired skewed and biased conceptions of Christianity? The answer is simple.

It's because you and I have allowed it to happen.

But enough is enough. Ray Thorne writes, "If we Christians don't continue to share the gospel and push the envelope, the envelope will close in on us. If we maintain a 'silent witness', there will be no witness, and Christianity will die in America."

As Christians we can no longer stand silently aside, while heresy flourishes. We can no longer keep the good news of Christ quiet, while the world proclaims its own twisted version of the gospel. We can no longer tolerate such tolerance. You and I have lived lifelessly for long enough.

"A thirty-eight-year-old man from Princeton, West Virginia, made an emergency 911 call in October 1992 to complain about gunshot wounds—three of them. Paramedics arrived and discovered the man had accidentally shot himself three times in the right foot—each with a different gun he was cleaning. According to the Sheriff's Deputy L. R. Catron, the man claimed the first shot from the .32-caliber handgun he was cleaning didn't hurt so he went on to clean the second gun, a .38-caliber pistol. When that one went off and shot him in the foot, it 'stung a little, but not too bad.' However, it was only when his third gun, a .357, fired and hit him in the foot that he decided to call 911..."[53]

How many more gunshot wounds to the heart can Christianity suffer? How many more scars can our souls bear? How much more will we take before we take a stand?

Christ said, *"All men will hate you because of Me, but he who stands firm to the end will be saved."*[54] For that reason, I believe we are each faced with a choice. Given the religious climate of America today, I believe you and I have two alternatives. We can either live our lives as congenial Christians, continuing to bathe in the lifeless tolerance that has enveloped American Christianity. Or else we can stand up and stand strong for what we believe to be true.

If you did you'd be amazed how many people are waiting—desperately—to follow you to Christ. You would trade congeniality for sincere love. You would trade mediocrity for passion. And most of all, you would take the first step toward the kind of life you were intended to live.

I warn you though, on the day of your funeral, you may not be described as having been merely "nice."

BURIED ALIVE: A DISCUSSION ON OVERCOMING THE "SEVEN LIFELESS SINS"

What I, _____ *, believe:*
           (Insert Your Name Here)

_____
_____
_____
_____
_____

Chapter 2

Tolerance
Fundamentalism

Fundamentalism

"You turned my wailing into dancing; You removed my sackcloth and clothed me with joy."[55]

— King David

"Don't worry about what you don't know
Life's a dance
You learn as you go."

— John Michael Montgomery, "Life's a Dance"

"Except for the point, the still point,
There would be no dance,
And there is only the dance."

— T. S. Eliot

In the last chapter we discussed the dangers of tolerance and the way its epidemic levels have ravaged contemporary Christianity. But that was only one side of the issue. That was only half of the story.

And so, just as the gospels juxtapose grace with works and mercy with justice, it seems only fitting to follow our last discussion on the dangers of tolerance with a plea for it…

To Dance with the Divine

I was still in grade school when it happened, it was at my best friend's birthday party, and it was with my first big crush. I don't remember whether she asked me or I asked her. I don't even remember the song. All I remember is how very nervous I was.

After all, I had never slow danced with a girl before.

My palms were sweaty and my breathing was labored, and as I

ushered her out onto the dance floor the only thing I could think of was the unthinkable. — I was scared of stepping on her toes!

Oh, that would be horrible. I would be embarrassed. She may be injured. And worst of all, she might think I was as bad of a dancer as I really was.

But then I got an idea. It was a brilliant solution. A stroke of genius. *I decided not to lift my feet.*

After all, there was no way her toe could slip beneath mine if I never lifted my feet off the ground. There was no risk of her being injured if I just kept my feet planted. And so, that was my answer. I would just keep my feet firmly on the ground, sway my hips back and forth a little, and she would never know the difference.

The only problem was since I never lifted my feet we never moved our location. Since I kept my feet planted we remained in the exact same spot for the entire song. I was beaming with satisfaction. Meanwhile, she was wishing she'd stayed seated over on the girls' side of the dance floor.

…I never have figured out why she wouldn't dance with me again that night.

†

The Christian life was intended to be unbridled and free. It is synonymous with pleasure and wonder and hope. It demands laughter and love and clumsy mistakes. It offers purpose and beauty and the life you've always wanted.

But like me and the first time I danced with a girl, I fear many of us are missing the point. We may sway our hips back and forth a little by going to church on Sunday and smiling to our neighbors Monday through Saturday. Yet our view of Christian living is so far from what Christ intended that we are missing the divine dance entirely.

As a result, many of us are far from becoming "congenial Christians." Instead we are modern day Pharisees.

Never mind the passion. Never mind the enthusiasm. Never mind the heart and the soul, the love and the desire. Rather, we are told, "Don't do this, don't do this, and certainly don't do this. — Then you will be a good Christian."

However, holiness is not defined by rules or regulations. (More on this in the next chapter.) And Christianity is not a futile attempt at perfection. Christ's teachings are intended to make us joyous and loving people, not judgmental or guilt ridden.

In fact, Jesus specifically instructed certain people to *defy* the dogmatic laws of His time.[56] And Paul asked in his letter to the Colossians, *"Since you died with Christ to the basic principles of this world, why, as though you still belonged to it, do you submit to its rules: 'Do not handle! Do not taste! Do not touch!'"?*[57]

With such a fundamental and legalistic mindset Christianity becomes just another religion. God becomes a killjoy. And we become hostages to our own legalizations.

†

Take the issue of alcohol for instance. No where in the Bible does it say we mustn't drink. It says not to be a drunkard, of course[58]. But one glass of wine is a far cry from drunken debauchery. After all, Jesus drank![59] Yet some fundamental Christians have made it such a taboo that today we are told we may "hurt our witness" by doing it. In essence, we may hurt our witness by doing *nothing wrong*.

How ironic.

How sad.

It seems that we have become more concerned with our own formulas than the actual teachings of Christ. We have become more focused on cultural sin than on what the Bible truly says. In the end, we've come to overlook the most important command of love and demonized acts that Christ never even mentioned.

"See to it that no one takes you captive through hollow and deceptive philosophy, which depends on human tradition and the basic principles of this world rather than on Christ."[60]

"Does God give you His Spirit and work miracles among you because you observe the law, or because you believe what you heard?"[61]

"These people honor me with their lips, but their hearts are far from me. They worship me in vain; their teachings are but rules taught by men."[62]

"Therefore do not let anyone judge you by what you eat or drink, or with regard to a religious festival, a New Moon celebration or a Sabbath day. These are a shadow of the things that were to come; the reality, however, is found in Christ."[63]

"Christ is the end of the law."[64]

"Let them praise His name with dancing."[65]

You see, fundamentalism means we move through this life with a stiff neck and held breath. It means we become more concerned with what we're separated from than what we're separated for. It means we grit our teeth and work with all our might to reach perfection.—Or at least to present ourselves as perfect to others.

Christianity means that we dance. Natural and free. Wild and true.

Stepping on our own feet at times. Falling flat on our face at others. But then humbly allowing Christ to pick us up, and trying it all over again.

The Greatest Fundamental

I used to wonder why God only gave Moses Ten Commandments. What about smoking? What about R-rated movies? What about liberal talk radio?

Clearly it was some kind of mistake. I mean, how can He expect us all to be perfect without precise parameters? How can He expect us all to be exactly the same without more detailed directives?

Luckily, Jesus came along. Surely He'd set things straight. Surely He'd fill in the gaps for us and straighten everyone else out. But instead He *shortened* the law. He cut to the heart like never before, leaving no room for mistake. He said, *"Love."*

In fact, when asked what the most important commandment was Jesus said, *"The most important one is this:...Love the Lord your God with all your heart and with all your soul and with all your mind and with all your strength. The second is this: Love your neighbor as yourself. There is no commandment greater than these."*[66]

Could He be any clearer?

Paul also said in his letter to the Romans, *"The commandments, 'Do not commit adultery,' 'Do not murder,' 'Do not steal,' 'Do not covet,' and whatever other commandments there may be, are summed up in this one rule: 'Love you neighbor as yourself.'"*[67]

BURIED ALIVE: A DISCUSSION ON OVERCOMING THE "SEVEN LIFELESS SINS"

I love the way Paul put that: "Whatever other commandments there may be." He understood human nature so well. He knew the inherent way we tack on rule after rule, formulating our own absolute theologies. So he said, point blank, forget it. Let it go. Don't worry about all that other stuff you don't know—*all that stuff you were never intended to know.*

Instead, love.

"Above all, love each other deeply."[68]

"The entire law is summed up in a single command: 'Love your neighbor as yourself.'"[69]

"All men will know that you are my disciples, if you love one another."[70]

"The only thing that counts is faith expressing itself through love."[71]

"And now these three remain: faith, hope and love. But the greatest of these is love."[72]

"If I speak in the tongues of men and angels, but have not love, I am only a resounding gong or clanging cymbal."[73]

"If I give all I possess to the poor and surrender my body to the flames, but have not love, I gain nothing."[74]

"If I have a faith that can move mountains, but I have not love, I am nothing."[75]

"live a life of love, just as Christ loved us."[76]

"Whoever does not love does not know God, because God is love."[77]

"This is the message you heard from the beginning: We should love one another."[78]

"Do everything in love."[79]

✝

From time to time I actually hear Christians brag about being fundamental. They brag about believing the Bible's literal truth and strictly adhering to its code of conduct. Yet sadly, it seems that these very same people, with their narrow theologies and pious demeanor, often overlook the greatest fundamental of all.

In truth, it is *love* that Christ spoke of again and again. It is *love* that Paul wrote about over and over. Everything else in life is a mere stepping stone along the road to this greater goal[80].

Honestly, I believe that God had rather have us cussing like sailors than gossiping like most church goers I know. But it seems as if the enemy has so exploited the importance of surface change that he has prolonged true, inner change. He has so successfully promoted the trivial that he has kept us from the essential.

In Light of Love

In light of Christ's teachings I am often left to wonder where all the love is in our nation today. Yesterday I walked into a local bookstore and found a dozen books, (mostly in the Christian section,) on why homosexuality is wrong and how we should deny "them" their rights. But as I stood there skimming the titles I couldn't help but wonder: Where are all the books on why and how we should *love* them?

For every book written on why homosexuality is a sin there should be twenty written on why we must love and accept and look first to the plank in our own eye. Yet it seems we have gotten off track. We have lost our focus on what truly matters. As a result, there is an ever thinning line between truth and discrimination, righteous anger and bigotry.

I realize that homosexuality is a hot topic of ethical debate in America today. Yet that is the precise reason why we as Christians should be reaching out with hands of kindness and sympathy. That is the precise reason why we must learn to love. After all, if Jesus were here today what do you think He would be doing? Who do you think He would be eating dinner with tonight, at the uproar of modern day Pharisees?

BURIED ALIVE: A DISCUSSION ON OVERCOMING THE "SEVEN LIFELESS SINS"

I also realize that this is the one issue I should avoid discussing at all cost. I can write all day long about loving widows and orphans and even telemarketers, but the very mention of homosexuals takes this conversation too far for many Christians. Yet again, that is the precise reason why we as Christians *should* be discussing it. That is the precise reason why we must let loose of our fundamental prejudices.

†

I can almost see the Pharisees pointing their fingers with one hand and gripping their stones in the other. I can almost see the adulterous woman, disgraced and ashamed, curled up at Jesus' feet. I can almost see Christ writing with his finger in the sand, saying, *"If any one of you is without sin, let him be the first to throw a stone at her."*[81]

It is eerie how closely today's reality parallels this two thousand year old story from Scripture. In many ways little has changed. Maybe it is time things did.

Don't misunderstand me. You can disagree with me if you like, but please don't misunderstand what I am trying to say. The point is not that homosexuality should be accepted and that we should all succumb to the lifeless sin of tolerance. After all, even in this Biblical story of Christ and the adulterous woman He concluded by instructing her, *"Go now and leave your life of sin."*[82]

No, the point is not that homosexuals are sinless.

The point is that *no one* is sinless.

You and I may not suffer from the vice of homosexuality, but what about other sins? According to Scripture homosexuality is wrong, but having said that…So is greed. So is lust. So is jealousy. So is grumbling. So is gluttony. So is vanity. So is selfishness. So is adultery. So is judging. So is dishonesty. So is pride. So is envy. So is resentment. So is cheating. So is hatred. So is hostility. So is bitterness. So is arrogance. So is over indulgence. So is disloyalty. So is deceit. So is conceit. So is extravagance. So is theft. So is pornography….I'll stop there before this becomes the longest and most depressing paragraph ever written.

Again, the obvious point is that I don't see anyone protesting, proposing legislation, or writing books on why we should alienate and deny the rights of those who habitually indulge in any of *these* sins.

So, rather than using our faith as a means to call the sin of others into light perhaps it is time we started using it as a means to love. Perhaps it is time we stopped using Christ as a wedge and started seeing Him as a bridge. Perhaps it is time we put aside the stones, along with our pride, and picked up our feet to dance.

Love as an End

It took me half my life to realize the value of love. — To *truly* realize, I mean. I had thought the only way to grow in Christ was to be regimented and disciplined. I had thought the only way to glorify God was to make followers out of skeptics and to build His body of believers.

But over the years my fiancée Brecca has taught me to love as an end, not merely as a means. As a result I have (almost) learned to love without an agenda. Many Christians today seem to need the same realization.

Don't reach out to someone so that you can bring them to church. Reach out to someone.

Don't befriend someone so that you can share Christ with them. Befriend someone.

Don't show compassion so that they may see the love of Christ. Show compassion.

If in the end they come to church with you, or you find the opportunity to share your faith with them, then by all means do so. After all, as a Christian that would be the most natural and loving thing you could do. But in the meantime, love them for who they are. Love them despite themselves. Love them *unconditionally*, as you and I are called to do.

No facades.

No agendas.

No schemes or strategies or tricks or conspiracies.

For as it turns out, love is what it truly means to follow Christ. Love is what it truly means to be Christian. And love is what it truly means to glorify God.

As it turns out, everything else is trivial.

BURIED ALIVE: A DISCUSSION ON OVERCOMING THE "SEVEN LIFELESS SINS"

Trivial Theologies or Old Highway 91

When I was very young I only saw things in black and white, and I only understood this world in a matter of extremes. I actually thought glasses made blind people see and I thought hospitals brought dead people back to life. I didn't seem to understand that there were people who could see, just not very well. It had never crossed my mind that there were living people who just weren't all that healthy.

I will never forget walking along Old Highway 91, a mile or two from my childhood home, when my older brother corrected my defective thinking. With the tough love of a big brother he looked me in the eyes and said, "What are you, an idiot?"

I tell you this because I sometimes still find myself seeing life in black and white. I sometimes still need the tough love of a Christian friend. Whether it be from my brother or my mother, my friends or my fiancée, I sometimes still need someone to correct my defective thinking.

Sometimes, I think we all do.

✝

This is true because we all have our own theology. Whether we're Catholic or Baptist, atheist or agnostic, we all have our own way of viewing and understanding this world in which we live. Sadly though, we also have an inclination to see our own personal theology as the one absolute true theology. We have a tendency to see our own way as the only way.

The obvious problem with this is that God transcends any possible understanding of Him. God is bigger than any tidy little package of beliefs that we try cramming Him into. And any metaphor we use to describe Him is merely that: a metaphor. C. S. Lewis echoed this same sentiment decades ago. Entitled *Footnote to All Prayers* he writes:

> He whom I bow to only knows to whom I bow
> When I attempt the ineffable Name, murmuring Thou…
>
> Thus always, taken at their word, all prayers blaspheme
> Worshipping with frail images a folk-lore dream

And all men are idolaters, crying unheard
To a deaf idol, if Thou take them at their word.[83]

This is why God's reply to Moses' question, "Who should I say sent me?" is so fitting. In response God doesn't try talking about His justice, love, compassion or wisdom. God doesn't even attempt to describe Himself for He knows better than to try to explain the unexplainable. Rather, God responds simply by saying, *"I AM WHO I AM."*[84]

I don't know about you, but I still haven't figured out how to make my VCR stop flashing. How on earth, then, do you or I have the audacity to think we've figured out our God? Why on earth do we presume to comprehend the countless complexities and infinite intricacies of our Lord? Where do we even begin to explain the unexplainable *I AM?* Tony Campolo articulates this point perfectly in *Adventures in Missing the Point.* He writes:

> "God is greater than any theology or system of ideas we come up with about God. God is not defined by our systems, by our theologies—not even by our firm convictions about him or her. Yes, *or her*—for God also transcends anything we think we know about masculinity and femininity. Check your New Testament Greek: against the masculine God the Father and Son, the Holy Spirit is referred to in the feminine gender. Even the Trinity defies the systematic packaging that theologies try to give it."[85]

The point is not that God is feminine. As Campolo says, God transcends anything we think we know about gender. The point, rather, is that *your theology's wrong*. I can write those words with such assurance because *no one* has the perfect theology. Not you. Certainly not me. Not even your favorite television evangelist.

We currently see but a portion of the picture and we currently understand but a fraction of that which is infinitely beyond ourselves. Someday we will see the whole image. And I expect it will shock us as much as Jesus' first coming did the people of that time. But until then we have only a poor reflection of an eternal truth.

If you doubt my words then inspect Paul's. For he is who I just paraphrased:

*BURIED ALIVE: A DISCUSSION ON OVERCOMING THE
"SEVEN LIFELESS SINS"*

"…we know in part and we prophecy in part, but when perfection comes, the imperfect disappears…Now we see but a poor reflection as in a mirror; then we shall see face to face. Now I know in part; then I shall know fully, even as I am fully known."[86]

The Reality of Relativity

In its attempt to combat the current epidemic of relativism—as we discussed in the last chapter—it seems that American Christianity often denies and resists its existence at all. As a result denominations outline their theologies in black and white, and we the congregations fall prey to thinking that our own theology is flawless and complete. But if God is beyond our comprehension then it is a very dangerous thing to over simplify and absolutize our beliefs.

For that reason we must learn to accept the reality of relativity *within* the absolute framework of Christianity.

Jesus Christ, revealed to us through Holy Scripture, is the sinless Son of God whose atoning sacrifice serves to offer abundant life and eternal salvation to anyone who acknowledges Him as their Lord. That is the undeniable belief of Christianity. But as far as I can see, that is where the absolutes end.

What about the role of women in church?[87]
What about homosexuality and the way we've handled it?[88]
What about losing salvation?[89]
What about evolution and the age of our universe?[90]
What about divorce and remarriage, in light of what Scripture teaches about adultery?[91]
What about infant death and salvation for those with severe mental retardation?[92]
What about speaking in tongues?[93]
What about other religious traditions such as baptism, communion, and circumcision?[94]
What about predestination?[95]
What about spiritual warfare?[96]
What about animal rights and caring for the environment?[97]
What about caring for impoverished people and nations?[98]
What about rewards in heaven?[99]
What about gun control and capital punishment?[100]
What about prayer and whether or not our words affect a sovereign God?[101]

What about birth control, stem cell research and medically assisted pregnancies?[102]
What about Bible interpretation?[103]
What about Israel, the Jews, and the fate of God's chosen people?[104]
What about the end times?[105]
What about suffering, and the fact that a God of love allows it?[106]
What about people who die without ever hearing the good news of Christ?[107]

You see, there are literally *thousands* of theological issues within Christianity that remain debatable. *Thousands* in which there are sincere, seeking Christians on both sides of the fence.

Do you or I have the perfect, definitive theology? Do you or I have all the right answers to all these debatable issues? Of course not. Why then do we so often pretend that we do?

Instead of developing and defending our own absolute theologies we must admit that we can never wrap our mind around God. — Let alone wrap God around our finger. After all, we *all* believe in relativity to a degree.

†

The very mention of Christianity and relativity in the same sentence is shocking to many Christians. It is much like the earlier mention of homosexuality alongside Christ's commandment to love.

However, consider the basic belief that Jesus is the only way to God. If you hold this to be true then it is an obvious conclusion that anyone who fails to accept Him as their Lord and Savior is to be condemned. In fact, if I tried to argue against this I'd probably be labeled a heretic by some.

Oddly though, I know very few Christians who actually believe this. I know very few Christians who would condemn a person with a severe mental handicap to hell for never having accepted Jesus. I don't know of any Christians who'd condemn an infant that dies at birth to eternal damnation. You see we all believe in relativity to one degree or another.

Another compelling example of this can be found in the sixteenth chapter of Mark. After His death and resurrection Jesus appeared to the eleven remaining disciples. He first rebuked them for their lack of faith and for their stubbornness. He then instructed them by saying,

BURIED ALIVE: A DISCUSSION ON OVERCOMING THE "SEVEN LIFELESS SINS"

"Go into all the world and preach the good news to all creation. Whoever believes and is baptized will be saved, but whoever does not believe will be condemned."[108]

Often described as the "great commission," these words are commonly used by fundamental Christians to confirm their sternly outlined theologies. However, these very same Christians seem to have never read the following two verses! Jesus continues by saying:

> *"And these signs will accompany those who believe: In my name they will drive out demons; they will speak in new tongues, they will pick up snakes with their hands; and when they drink deadly poison, it will not hurt them at all; they will place their hands on sick people, and they will get well."*[109]

Again, it seems that most all of us support theological relativity to one degree or another, whether we realize it or not. How else can you explain the way we canonize Jesus' first comments about missionary work and the need to believe, while dismissing His last comments about driving out demons and drinking deadly poison? Jesus said the two comments in one single breath, yet we embrace one and ignore the other. The red letters of Scripture never stop, yet our inadequate theologies do.

†

It seems that many of us are so frightened of uncertainty that we've removed all room for spiritual growth.

But I don't think we should have to pretend before others to have all the answers, in order to convince ourselves that we have faith. What we must realize is we do not know all of life's answers for sure because *we are not intended to know for sure*. And there are so many options and opinions within the central framework of Christianity because *there are suppose to be so many options and opinions*.

> *"One man's faith allows him to eat anything, but another man...eats only vegetables...One man considers one day more sacred than another; another man considers every day alike. Each one should be fully convinced in his own mind...Therefore let us stop passing judgment on one another...whatever you believe about these things keep between yourself and God."*[110]

53

Again, I am not doubting or questioning the truth of Jesus Christ. There is nothing I am surer of in this world. However, I believe it is time we as Christians felt free to think and reason and ponder and consider and contemplate and meditate and question and wonder *within* that boundary of truth.

I believe it is time we embraced a spirituality deep enough to cause doubt. I believe it is time we embraced a God big enough to cause mystery. And I believe it is time the church allowed us to.

For as Christians we must forever be confident in God. But we must never grow self-confident in our own thoughts or theologies about God.

The Eternal Canvas

My good friend Chase says that God is like a billion brushstrokes dancing across an eternal canvas. Since the character of God can never be grasped or comprehended by the limited understanding of one single mind, only when viewed as a whole do our theologies even begin to touch His true character. He says that only together is the picture formed.

I think that's the most beautiful depiction of God I've ever heard.

From Catholics to Protestants, liberals to conservatives, solemn to charismatic, pious to casual, we all have something to offer the cause of Christ. We have all been given a special passion or ability that expresses something unique about our Maker. That is the beauty made possible through the New Covenant of Christ, for Christianity is not a mold, but a mosaic. Or to use an illustration from Paul's epistles, Christians are like different parts of one body:

> *"For we were all baptized by one Spirit into one body—whether Jews or Greeks, slave or free—and we were all given the one Spirit to drink…Now the body is not made up of one part but of many…If the whole body were an eye, where would the sense of hearing be? If the whole body were an ear, where would the sense of smell be? But in fact God has arranged the parts in the body, every one of them, just as He wanted them to be…and each one of you is a part of it."*[111]

BURIED ALIVE: A DISCUSSION ON OVERCOMING THE "SEVEN LIFELESS SINS"

As it turns out, our own perspectives and understandings can never stand alone for they were never intended to. But when we see them as one body then we begin to live and grow healthy spiritual lives. We move beyond the fundamentalist pit of lifelessness. We pick up our feet to dance.

On the other hand, when we merge our own trivial theologies with the absolute truth of Jesus Christ then Christianity becomes some sort of package deal. We expect everyone to think just as we do, squashing out all room for diversity. And unbelievers think that if they place their faith in Jesus Christ they'll have to cut their hair, stop recycling, and fall in love with the Republican Party. As a result we often push unbelievers away who see Christianity as a cookie cutting religion and we wring all the color out of new believers.

But in reality it only makes sense that our relationships with God would be so different and diverse. Consider a friend and your relationship with him or her. Think of the words you would use to describe them and the relationship you share. Now, think of how others would view and describe that very same person. What words may they use to describe their relationship? You would each be speaking of the same friend but because perspectives and relationships vary so would your words and understandings.

In the same way, if we have acknowledged Christ as our Savior and allow Him to work in our lives then we have been made part of His body. Yet each of our relationships with Him will be inherently personal and different.

To some He is a comforter (2 Corinthians 1:3). To some He is a refuge (Psalm 18:2). To some He is a father figure (Luke 23:34). To some He is a judge (Hebrews 9:27). To some He is a strengthener (Philippians 4:13). To some He is a warrior (Exodus 15:3). To some He is a teacher (John 13:13). To some He is a healer (Psalm 147:3). To some He is a friend (James 2:23).

But as long as He is Lord to us all, that is all that matters.

†

I believe this is such an important understanding—the beauty of varying perspectives—because without it you and I are left void of the lessons this world has to offer.

Consider such concerns as gender equality and environmental stewardship. Over the years liberal Christians and even unbelievers have championed these issues. Meanwhile, the contemporary church has sadly ignored and even contested them. As a result, an "environmental Christian" or a "Christian feminist" has come to sound almost contradictory.

But why?

In light of Scripture, why aren't Christians on the front line of the environmental movement?[112] Why do Christians so often stand in the way of gender equality?[113] Why can't these concerns be an expression of our Christian faith rather than an opposition to it? Why can't we stand firm on our traditional moral values while pressing forward on progressive social issues?

Could it be that both liberals *and* conservatives have something to offer the cause of Christ? Could it be that both liberals *and* conservatives are amiss on a number of things?

Bono, the lead singer of U2, expresses this point perfectly. He comments on the need for unity and understanding by saying, "The Left mocks the Right. The Right knows its right. Two ugly traits. How far should we go to try to understand each other's point of view? Maybe the distance grace covered on the cross is a clue."[114]

The apostle Paul also writes in his letter to Colosse: *"Let the peace of Christ rule in your hearts, since as members of one body you were called to peace. And be thankful."*[115] And again, in his letter to Titus he writes: *"avoid foolish controversies and genealogies and arguments and quarrels about the law, because these are unprofitable and useless."*[116]

You see, if we truly want to live this life of ours to the full then you and I will let loose of our fundamental entrapments. We will overlook divisional stereotypes, welcoming our differences. And we will seek to learn from other perspectives.

We won't do this by talking down to others, but by talking with them. We will toss out our agendas and seek first to love. We will preach less and listen more.

For no one wants to be told how to live. They want to be understood, known and valued. Ironically, it is only then that they may listen to your words. Even learn. *And so will you.*

After all, in the walk of life we are all unfinished.

Unfinished Christians

He didn't have a name. Or at least not one that anyone knew. He had only a shriveled hand.

And so, the no-named-man with a shriveled hand was astonished one day to hear someone calling out to him. He turned to see who had spoken, but saw only strange faces. One of these faces peered directly at him with wild eyes; eyes of life and love, passion and truth. Yet the no-named-man with a shriveled hand did not recognize Him. So he dropped his eyes to the ground and turned back around.

Then suddenly the wild eyed Man spoke again. He called the man's name once more and said, "Stand up. Come here to Me."

The Pharisees watched from a distance, waiting for a reason to accuse Jesus. They waited for anything they may use against Him. They waited for a reason to kill. They needn't wait long, for as the Pharisees were plotting how they might destroy Jesus was plotting how He would restore.

The two men stood side by side; one wild eyed, the other timid and shy. Then Jesus said, "Stretch out your hand."

The no-named-man with a shriveled hand hesitated. He looked down at the hand, curled up and tucked away deep into the folds of his robe. To him it was a physical symbol of shame. According to the religious laws of the time he had committed some sin to deserve such a disgrace. He did not want to expose it here, now, before such a gathering.

He looked back at Jesus. He looked into His eyes. There was no denying those eyes. There was no resisting their call. And so he removed his hand. Small. Bony. Coiled. He stretched it out for all to see, closing his eyes and hiding his face, laying himself bare before the Lord. And in doing so his hand was restored. Whole. Strong. Healthy.

The crowd gasped with amazement. The Pharisees teemed with jealousy. And the mended man, once known only by his deformity, danced with joy as his name echoed through out the heavens for all eternity. (Luke 6:1-11)

✝

During Jesus' life the greatest opposition He faced was not from the pagans, but from the Pharisees. They were jealous of Christ's influence. They were insulted by His teachings. They were infuriated by His love.

Even when Christ *healed* a man they were too concerned with their law to see their Lord.

That is the risk we run with extreme fundamentalism. Instead of laying ourselves bare before the Lord we pretend to have all the answers. Instead of looking at our own deficiencies we eagerly point out the faults of others. Instead of humbly admitting that we're unfinished Christians we hide away, cover up, gloss over, or ignore the parts of life that don't fit into our own theologies. In the end we sound less like Christ Jesus and more like the religious leaders who killed Him.

Of course there is risk at the other extreme too. In the midst of his writings about love and our newfound freedom from the law Paul also writes, *"Be careful, however, that the exercise of your freedom does not become a stumbling block to the weak…'Everything is permissible for me'—but not everything is beneficial."*[117]

After all, if secular music and Harry Potter books really aren't as evil as we've been told they are then where should the line be properly drawn? If we begin to ask questions then when will the questions end? And if we begin to think for ourselves then where will such thinking lead us?

Ultimately we may move into dangerous, sloping ground. We may be pulled beyond the safe perimeters of our personal theologies. We may step on some toes.

But then again, out among the risk and danger is always where true life is found. It seems in the end that we must ask ourselves which is more costly: to risk seeking God's face unbridled and free, or to risk not to?

Live to Love, Dare to Dance

For some of you this chapter has been a breath of fresh air. For years your spirit has been smothered. Your soul has all but suffocated. Finally you feel allowed to breathe. But for others I am still chipping at a cold wall of resistance you've erected between "my type" and yourself.

I know because I have been there before.

That is the reason why this chapter is so close to my heart. Not long ago I began reading the likes of Donald Miller and the late Michael Yaconelli, among others. As I read I couldn't help but protest silently in the margins. I even had scripture to support my narrow views.

Some of the time.

Of course, when I did I usually had to ignore a dozen other scriptures that challenged or even contradicted my own viewpoint. But nonetheless, I had scripture. Nonetheless, I was right.

But slowly I learned—mostly the hard way—that Christianity is not about being right. It is not about having all the answers. It is not about

*BURIED ALIVE: A DISCUSSION ON OVERCOMING THE
"SEVEN LIFELESS SINS"*

having arrived. Such thoughts miss the whole point of this chapter. They miss the whole point of Christ's teachings.

In fact, true Christianity is the continual understanding that we *haven't* all the answers. It is the continual understanding that we *haven't* arrived. For just as the first step toward salvation is immersed in the humble realization that we are imperfect and incomplete, every step after that is paved by the same humility.

†

Sir Winston Churchill once said, "Men occasionally stumble over the truth, but most of them pick themselves up and hurry on as if nothing had happened."

So, if this chapter has caused you to raise a few questions or lift a few eyebrows, then good. If it has challenged you or stretched you or caused some doubt, then even better.

Just don't hurry on so quickly.

Stay a while. Open your mind. Enjoy the music. Dare to dance.

After all, God is not some sort of judgmental watchdog. He is not a killjoy or a spoilsport or a party pooper. *God is dancing*. And He is saving the next dance for you…

> To dance
> In rhythmic motion
> With the grace of a whisper
> With the roar of an ocean
> Now is the time
> Your hand in Mine
> This is your time
> Your time
> To dance

Afterthought: Recommended Readings for Fundamentalism

1. *Blue Like Jazz*
   by Donald Miller
2. *Adventures in Missing the Point*
   by Brian McLaren & Tony Campolo
3. *Harry Potter*
   by J. K. Rowling
4. *Searching for God Knows What*
   by Donald Miller
5. *The Emerging Church*
   by Dan Kimball
6. *Dangerous Wonder*
   by Michael Yaconelli
7. *Messy Spirituality*
   by Michael Yaconelli
8. *The Post-Evangelical*
   by Dave Tomlinson
9. *A New Kind of Christian*
   by Brian McLaren
10. *A Generous Orthodoxy*
    by Brian McLaren
11. *Making Sense of Church*
    by Spencer Burke
12. *The Church in Emerging Culture*
    edited by Leonard Sweet
13. *God's Politics*
    by Jim Wallis
14. *Sojourners Magazine*
    edited by Jim Wallis
15. *The New Testament*
    by God (kind of)

Chapter 3

Tolerance
Fundamentalism
Compromise

Compromise

"*If My people, who are called by My name, will humble themselves and pray and seek My face and turn from their wicked ways, then will I hear from heaven and will forgive their sin and will heal their land.*"[118]
—God

"No message could have been any clearer
If you wanna make the world a better place
Take a look at yourself and then make a change"
—Michael Jackson, 'Man in the Mirror'

"We must be the change we wish to see in the world."
—Mahatma Gandhi

With the directions she gave him he arrived at her house later that night. As always, my dad was right on time. He walked up to the door and knocked. Then he was ushered in and offered a chair. Evidently his date wasn't ready yet, so he sat silently and began watching an episode of Gunsmoke.

Five minutes…

Ten minutes…

My dad continued to wait patiently as the episode ended and another episode came on. He craned his neck to look down the hallway, but there was no Sarah to be seen. He looked around the room at his hosts, but their eyes remained fixed on the television screen.

Twenty minutes…

Twenty five minutes…

My dad grew more and more restless. He shifted in his seat. He fidgeted anxiously. But still, he waited.

Thirty minutes...
Forty minutes...
When the second episode of Gunsmoke finally drew to an end so did my dad's patience. He had waited politely, but he could no longer contain himself. He finally broke the silence.

"So, is Sarah about ready?" He asked.

"Sarah?" The couple looked at each other and then back at my father with confused faces, "Sarah lives two houses down."

They didn't have a daughter named Sarah. They didn't have a daughter at all.

My dad had been in the wrong house the entire time.

Ranting About Armageddon

Can I be honest with you for a moment? The story you just read has little to do with this chapter. Or at least, it does now.

You see, I had originally written this entire chapter on the premise that our world was getting worse. I used the story you just read to show just how much the times have changed. After all, in today's world we would be more likely to lock a family member out of the house than to let a stranger in.

I even had a second story about my recent trip to Venice and the way this sinking city paralleled America's sinking morality. And I had another one about the time my great uncle poured motor oil all over his mother's fruitcake, illustrating the way we are all fruitcakes in the marinade of society.

It was all very brilliant. Very, very moving. You would have been tied up in knots and then left crying like a baby. I'm almost sure of it.

Not really.

In fact, when I read back over my own words they seemed a bit trite. My entire line of reasoning was cliché. The whole chapter seemed to be, well, *lifeless*.

That's because in recent years we've all heard the mantra of how bad things have gotten more times than we can remember. And we've heard enough ranting about Armageddon to keep us thoroughly paranoid and depressed until the day Jesus really does come back. I believe we've had enough scare tactics. I don't think we need anymore reminders or prophecies.

For that reason I've felt compelled to completely rewrite my original discussion on compromise. I've felt compelled to move beyond the "world is going to hell in a hand basket" rhetoric that I'm accustomed to hearing from the pulpit. I've felt compelled, instead, to discuss the *real* problem.

The Real Problem

I find it interesting as I read through Paul's epistles that in all of his writing he never once blamed the Roman government for his faults or transgressions. He never once used the persecution he and the early Christian church endured as an excuse for lifeless living. In fact, Paul did quite the opposite. He proclaimed himself the worst of sinners, and he took full responsibility for his actions. I believe we could learn a lot today from Paul's sense of accountability.

You see, it's easy for us as Christians to reflect on the past as if things were once perfect. It's easier still for us to blame the politicians and the media and the Hollywood role models for the way things are. However, *I believe the gravest mistake we as Christians make today is to play the role of the victim.*

As if we're pure and spotless vessels amidst a sea of iniquity, Christians condemn everything—outside of themselves—for the way things have gotten. We cast the guilt and then reminisce about how things used to be. We point our fingers and then snub our noses.

But to make blanket statements about how the world is falling apart and then sit back doing nothing is just useless. To over simplify reality and then turn our backs to it is simply ignorant. To blame society without taking responsibility is truly lifeless.

Tony Evans, the dynamic writer and speaker, comments on this fact by writing:

> "The tragedy today is not that sinners sin; that's what they're expected to do, since mankind was born in sin and shaped with iniquity (Psalm 51:5, Ephesians 2:1-3). The real tragedy is that the church as a whole has failed to act as salt and light in this society…It is not until Christians take the lead that the culture will have something to follow…until Christians change, the culture won't change, no matter how much we lament the violence and immorality and long for the good old days."[119]

†

The purpose of Christianity is not to critique or criticize this world in which we live. The purpose, rather, is to *change* it.

So instead of discussing society's sinking morality I think it's time Christians began discussing their own. Instead of debating over whether or not society is getting worse I think it's time we rose above such a line of reasoning all together. And instead of arguing I think it's time we began asking: *What am I going to do about it?*

If we did, then perhaps we would stop pointing fingers and start lending a hand. Perhaps we would stop casting blame and start taking responsibility. Perhaps we would stop discussing all the differences that have taken place and start making a difference ourselves.

For as Christians, the real problem is *not* this world's diminishing morals.

The real problem, it seems, is Christianity's contemporary response to them.

Being the Solution

The way that we too often look outside of ourselves, living passively rather than actively and reactively rather than proactively, is reflected even in the way we pray. My friend Chase is going through a difficult time right now with his girlfriend. And so, just last night I was praying for their situation. I was praying in a way much like you'd expect, "Lord be with Chase and Brit...Give them wisdom to make good decisions...Help them to find strength and comfort in You..."

Then suddenly I realized something, as if God were speaking directly to my heart. It wasn't audible, but more of a feeling, and if that feeling were put to words God would have said something like this:

> *"Jacob, thanks for talking with Me tonight. I love these times together of ours, and I love the way your heart is reaching out for Chase and Brit. But if I, being God and all, may offer a bit of advice:*

BURIED ALIVE: A DISCUSSION ON OVERCOMING THE "SEVEN LIFELESS SINS"

> *Perhaps you should move beyond praying for Me to help your friends. What I mean is, instead of asking Me to guide, strengthen, and comfort them why not ask Me how* you *can guide, strengthen and comfort them? Why not ask Me to use* you *in accomplishing what we both want done in their lives? Go ahead, Jacob, just ask Me. I'm longing to tell you…"*

As I lay there in bed considering what God had laid on my heart it all seemed so obvious. After all, Jesus didn't merely sit back, condemning the world and discussing how things needed to change. He engaged the world. He loved and embraced the world. He caused the change He saw needed to take place.

For that reason Christianity must stop casting blame and prophesizing Armageddon. Instead we must start taking responsibility for our own failings. And we must start making the change we wish to see in this world.

If we did that then maybe, just maybe, we would stop pretending to be the victims and start being the solution.

Casualties of Compromise

I will never forget bumping into Steve. I will never forget his words.

I had worked alongside Steve for years. Then one Sunday I brushed by him on my way out of church. When I looked up he met me with a smile and a handshake, and said, "Good to see you Jacob. I didn't know you where a Christian."

His words hurt.

He didn't intend for them to. I know he didn't. I know Steve. He was just making small talk, trying to welcome me to his church family, speaking what was on his mind. But as I shook his hand and returned his smile I couldn't help but think of what he'd said.

I had worked alongside Steve for *years*, yet he had no idea I was a Christian. I'm sure he knew what my favorite football team was, my favorite movies and music, even my political positions. Yet he had no idea who was my Lord.

As I walked back to my car I considered what this said about my spiritual life. After all, if I believed in God shouldn't my actions reflect it? If I was a Christian shouldn't people be able to tell?

I realized at that moment I was not living the life Christ had called me to. I had bought into the Christian propaganda I grew up hearing that said I was a victim. But in reality I was part of the problem. I was a casualty of compromise.

†

I've always thought it'd be nice if I could walk up to an unbeliever and show him or her a nice little chart saying, "Look, Christians are more loving, more forgiving, and more likely to get their taxes in on time." I have always thought that would be a very convincing testimony of the power of Christ.

But in reality it seems that the actions of Christians are often no different than the rest of this world. Despite what Romans 6:6-7 says, there is often no statistical difference between the lives of believers and unbelievers. (In fact, certain research has found that the divorce rates between born again Christians and unbelievers are virtually identical.[120])

These truths used to sadden, amaze and confuse me all at once. After all, if God really is who He says He is then shouldn't statistics reflect it? If Christ really is powerful enough to answer prayer then shouldn't I be able to make a chart that clearly shows it?

But then I realized the obviousness of it all: *There is often no statistical or visible difference in the lives of many Christians because there is often no statistical or visible difference in the way many Christians choose to live their lives.*

It's not that God isn't who He claims to be. It's that we don't always believe it. It's not that God isn't powerful enough to work in our lives. It's that you and I won't let Him.

You see, we can't pass the same judgments, repeat the same gossip and harbor the same resentment as the rest of this world, then still expect to be *"the salt of the earth."*[121] We can't surrender our beliefs, forfeit our character and sacrifice our integrity, then somehow expect to be *"the light of the world."*[122] Like me, on that Sunday I bumped into Steve, we cannot live as part of the problem and then somehow expect to be the solution.

In short, we cannot expect to live blessed lives when we refuse to live the kind of lives God blesses.

†

BURIED ALIVE: A DISCUSSION ON OVERCOMING THE
"SEVEN LIFELESS SINS"

All of this makes me think that maybe the reason Christians rant so much about Armageddon is because we don't want to draw any attention to the way we are living. It makes me think that maybe the reason we as Christians spend so much time emphasizing the eternal difference between heaven and hell is because we can't emphasize any difference in our lives.

[Insert Your Name Here]

King Belshazzar knew how to throw a party. He prepared enough food and gathered enough wine to feed over a 1000 people. Then he invited all of the aristocrats from there to Nineveh.

People started to arrive shortly before sundown. Most of them wanted to come fashionably late, but they couldn't wait. They couldn't contain their excitement. They wanted to get a good seat. And they certainly didn't want to miss anything.

Met at the gates by valets, servants, and ushers the guests were led into Belshazzar's enormous palace. Through a courtyard. Up some steps. Into a foyer. Down a corridor. Through another courtyard. Another corridor. And another. Finally, towering oak doors were swung open, leading into the grand banquet hall.

Vaulted ceilings soared overhead. Hundreds of candlelit chandeliers illuminated the place like constellations in the night sky. Rows of tables filled the room, crowned with silk, silver and china. The band was already struck up.

Before long the festivities were in full swing. There were comedians and jesters. There were dancers and acrobats. There were stories and jokes and laughter and tears.

Then just when the guests' stomachs had had all the food they could eat and their faces had had all the laughter they could bear, king Belshazzar proffered a special treat. With a regal snap of his fingers the king's servants emerged on cue. They marched into the hall one by one, carrying the temple goblets of Jerusalem.

Each guest took a cup and raised it for a toast. They mocked the God of Israel by toasting the gods of silver and gold. They toasted the gods of iron and stone. They toasted the…

Suddenly the music stopped. The guests sat motionless. The king grew pale.

The fingers of a human hand had appeared. They hung ghostly in the air, and then began to move purposefully on the wall. They wrote an inscription. Its meaning was cryptic, but the very sight left Belshazzar petrified.

Immediately the king called all of his astrologers and enchanters and all of the wise men of Babylonia. He promised authority and treasure to whoever could decipher the message. But no one was able. No one could interpret the riddled words on the wall.

Then, just when the situation seemed helpless, as the guests stood baffled and the king's knees grew weaker, his queen burst into the great banquet hall. Struggling to catch her breath, she exclaimed, "Don't be alarmed! Don't look so pale! There is a man in your kingdom by the name of Daniel who has the very spirit of God in him." (Daniel 5:1-11)

†

Imagine that: Daniel had not been in the king's court for years. He had not been welcome under the abhorrent rule of Belshazzar. Yet Daniel's reputation was renowned. He had not negotiated his morals or conceded to lifelessness. He had certainly not become a casualty of compromise. And so when a man of God was needed Daniel's name was called upon.

Now, imagine this: A party is thrown. God is defiled. The host becomes terrified. And then, from out of nowhere someone bursts in, "Don't be alarmed! Don't look so pale! There is someone in town named [insert your name here] who has the very spirit of God in them."

Would anyone say that about you or me?

Would they even think it?

By the day to day way we live our lives, would they have any reason to?

See God for More Details

Since I'm being so painfully honest with this chapter I should probably interrupt things again.

You see, at this point I had originally begun talking about holiness, and the need for you and I as Christians to live holy lives. Once more it was all very brilliant. It was kind of like *Gone with the Wind* meets *Star Wars* meets *Titanic*. You would have loved it.

BURIED ALIVE: A DISCUSSION ON OVERCOMING THE "SEVEN LIFELESS SINS"

The only problem was that I had no idea what I was writing about. I know there is a need for holiness. I know it's the call on each of our lives, and I know it's the only way we can ever truly overcome the lifelessness of compromise. This I know, for the Bible tells me so.

"But just as He who called you is holy, so be holy in all you do; for it is written: "Be holy, because I am holy.""[123]

"For God did not call us to be impure, but to live a holy life. Therefore, he who rejects this instruction does not reject man but God, who gives you his Holy Spirit."[124]

"I urge you to live a life worthy of the calling you have received."[125]

"Whatever happens, conduct yourselves in a manner worthy of the gospel of Christ."[126]

"Keep yourselves pure."[127]

"Do not conform any longer to the pattern of this world, but be transformed by the renewing of the mind."[128]

"Hate what is evil; cling to what is good."[129]

"God's temple is sacred, and you are that temple."[130]

"You are not your own; you were bought at a price. Therefore honor God with your body."[131]

"For we are the temple of the living God. As God has said: 'I will live with them and walk among them, and I will be their God, and they will be my people. Therefore come out from them and be separate, says the Lord.'"[132]

"Without holiness no one will see the Lord."[133]

Yet for the same reason I feel so qualified to write on the issue of lifelessness, I don't feel worthy even typing the word "holy." That label seems about as likely to describe my life as the title of Miss America. I don't know about you, but I identify more with Paul when he said, "What a wretched man I am!"[134]

That is, unless holiness means something very different than what many of us have come to think of today...

I wonder this because when I examine lives in scripture, the lives of righteous men like David and Moses and Noah and Abraham, I don't see perfection. Instead I see humanity tarnished by mistakes and inconsistencies, sincerity and authenticity. I see drunks and liars and adulterers and polygamists and cowards and even murderers. And so, stepping back to consider all of this makes me wonder whether we've been going about this whole issue of holiness all wrong.

Be that as it may, some people I know throw the concept of holiness around like it's a third grade spelling word. Preachers and teachers talk about it as if they themselves are living proof, and as if you and I should feel ashamed if we haven't yet reached this standard God has set for our lives.

From the way they talk you'd think holiness was something you could package and sell. But I don't think anyone can package something no one can fathom. And even if they could it would probably come with a disclaimer that read something like this:

> Holiness is a registered trademark of Jesus of Nazareth. Any attempt at repeating or imitating said trademark should be done with extreme caution. For a limited time only. Some restrictions apply. See God for more details.

In saying this I'm not trying to discredit the worth of purity. I believe that scripture is serious when it says holiness is a call on each of our lives. And so I believe holiness is truly a precious and priceless thing.

It's just that many Christians today seem confused by what holiness is. Many of us have no idea what we even mean when we say the word. As a result, I believe that we need a paradigm shift. We need to change our thinking entirely.

†

By definition holiness means to be "set apart, sanctified, consecrated, and dedicated." However—if I could have your attention please—that does *not* mean we must be flawless and solemn. It does *not* mean we must act like God.

Rather, it means being honest and sincere. It means allowing God to act through us.

There is an enormous difference between these two views. One means being pious, the other means being humble. One means we pretend to be perfect, the other means we admit that we are sinners. One means we try to act like saints, the other means we live the life God intended for us to live.

That's why men like David and Moses and Noah and Abraham where favored by God despite their utter, incessant failures. They weren't at all holy in the sense of perfection and flawlessness. Yet they were still four of the Godliest men to have ever walked this earth.

The legendary singer/songwriter Rich Mullins seems to agree. He once commented on the common misperceptions of holiness by saying, "I think many times we are afraid to drop our guard because we're afraid that people will think that we are spiritually fake. Well, the truth is that we are. And so are they. And we're all trying to fake each other out."[135]

I can't help but think of Rich's words when I imagine sitting around the Thanksgiving table with my family. Everyone is enjoying lively conversation, laughing at uncle Mackey's jokes, listening again to all of grandpa's favorite stories. Then someone is asked to pray, and suddenly the fun stops. Everyone become serious. Eyes closed. Heads bowed. Smiles are wiped away and giggles are hushed. The scene looks more like an army drill than an act of worship, as everyone erects some silly façade of what they believe holiness looks like.

But if you want to know what holiness truly is then look at a mother as she holds her newborn baby. Look at a couple as they exchange their wedding vows or celebrate their fiftieth anniversary. Look at a neighbor as he cares for a widowed woman.

That is what holiness truly is. You don't have to be serious and solemn and stuck up. You don't have to talk like you just stepped out of a King James Bible. You don't even have to buy a cabin in the mountains and live as a recluse, away from all of the sin and debauchery of the modern world. You certainly could, if that's what God has laid on your heart. But you don't have to.

Instead, humble yourself like king David did. Love your neighbor like Moses did. Seek truth like Noah did. And boldly follow God like Abraham did.

After all, if this world really is as bad as Christianity says it is then a life like that would be "set apart" indeed.

Step One: Not Proud

As it turns out, holiness is very different than the image many of us have grown up with in our heads. It is less about acting and more about living; less about perfection and more about sincerity. For that reason the path of genuine holiness begins in a place many of us often overlook entirely: *sin.*

> *"Sin is the monster we love to deny. It can stalk us, bite a slice out of our lives, return again and bite again, and even as we bleed and hobble, we prefer to believe nothing has happened. That makes sin the perfect monster, a man-eater that blinds and numbs its victims, convincing them that nothing is wrong and there is no need to flee, and then consumes them at its leisure."*[136]

Chase says that our society today is more interested in appearance than substance. We care more about looking slim and fit than we do about actually being healthy. We care more about appearing prosperous than we do about true financial stability. In the same way, he says that many Christians today care more about giving the impression that they are nice, pleasant people than they do about actually following Christ's teachings.

As a result many of us seek a sort of superficial sanctity. Rather than humbly addressing our sin nature we skip over this first step all together and try to put on 'instant holiness' as if it were a shirt and tie. We begin to act the way we think we should act. We try to talk the way we think we should talk. Our hearts are often in the right place, but in the end the act never lasts. In time the shirt is torn and the tie is tattered. And sooner or later we're back where we began, seeking 'instant holiness' all over again.

The obvious problem is that we are all sinners. Paul writes in his letter to the Romans, *"I know that nothing good lives in me, that is, in my sinful nature. For I have the desire to do what is good, but I cannot carry it out."*[137] He goes on to write that we've all fallen *short of the glory of God.*[138] For in truth, *there is no one righteous, not even one.*[139]

I actually find an odd comfort in this reality. By acknowledging and confessing my sin nature I find that I no longer have to act or pretend or lie or kid myself. And I realize that I am no longer on my own.

BURIED ALIVE: A DISCUSSION ON OVERCOMING THE "SEVEN LIFELESS SINS"

In fact, a few years ago Scott Huot and GW Brazier began a website called Notproud.com. Their website is an anonymous message board where people can secretively confess their sins, their shame and their regrets. The website has proved, above all else, that you and I are not alone in our transgressions...

2/17/04, at 10:32 pm
"I sometimes belittle other people in order to feel a flashy moment of intellectual superiority. In truth, I'm terrified. Of everything."

6/8/2003, at 10:45 pm
"I despise rich people, yet I aspire to be rich."

12/23/2000, at 12:21 am
"Anytime someone tries to give one of my friends attention, I automatically steal the spotlight away from them. I must be the center of attention. I must have all the love."

2/24/2004, at 10:02 pm
"My computers see more of me than my friends and family."

2/4/2004, at 4:22 am
"It pleases me to see happy people take a fall. I particularly like breakups and divorces."

11/23/2000, at 1:29 pm
"I can't even leave the house to buy a carton of milk without getting all teased and made-up. Then I spend close to an hour each night removing all the crap. I hate the routine, but you never know who might be looking."

12/16/03, at 1:18 am
"I have a serious drug problem. I have too much pride to ask for help. Pride is harder to overcome than the drugs themselves."

4/1/02, at 3:17 am
"My pride as a doctor led me to misdiagnose a patient, who then went blind as a result."

12/13/2002, at 12:17 pm
"My tombstone will read, A Life Not Lived."[140]

The reason we must realize and admit our own sin, like those who left these anonymous confessions, is because only then may we begin our life's journey toward true, Biblical holiness. God tells us in Scripture, "*I am the lord, who makes you holy.*"[141] So, true holiness is not about what you or I can do but rather about what He can do. Otherwise it wouldn't—it *couldn't*—be holiness.

Satan loves secrets. And the book of Proverbs tells us, "*He who conceals his sins does not prosper, but whoever confesses and renounces them finds mercy.*"[142] Therefore if we truly want to move beyond the lifeless entrapments of compromise we must first acknowledge our own shortcomings and confess our own failures, to both God and to one another.[143] We must give up the act and give it all to Him, even if that means we chuck the shirt and toss the tie.

For if the enemy is found in sins committed then the Lord is found in sins confessed.

Step Two: The Lure of Christ

Recent winters in the small mountain village had been harsh. Life was callous and cruel. Then one day rumors of a new home, rich in gold and flowing with honey, made there way to the hopeful villagers.

A band of men immediately set out to find this rumored land. They traveled across river and valley, through forest and desert, over ocean and mountain. Their journey lasted a lifetime, until one day they finally arrived. They looked up to see a beautiful land of lavish green. Then they looked down to see two paths separating them from this newfound paradise.

One path was wide and the other path was narrow. Upon the wide path stood a man in shadow. Upon the narrow path stood a Man in silence.

The shadowy gatekeeper immediately began to entice them with all the pleasures his path had to offer. He spoke to them of luscious food and drink. He spoke to them of illustrious riches. His lure was too great for any man to resist, and so one by one the men accepted his offer.

BURIED ALIVE: A DISCUSSION ON OVERCOMING THE "SEVEN LIFELESS SINS"

They walked along, eating and drinking and filling their pockets. But soon the wide, easy path grew more crooked and more treacherous. It turned, leading the men far away from the paradise of green they had been promised. It became so steep that they stumbled to the ground. In time the men became lost within its maze of passages. They staggered deeper and deeper into the darkness. They were unable to make it back the way they had come.

The other men saw the deceitfulness of this dark gatekeeper. They witnessed the treachery of his path. Yet the men still found themselves unable to resist its lure.

Some galloped their colts away from the wide passage, only to find themselves suddenly among its shadowy ruin. Others clenched their bodies to the roots of nearby trees. But the roots began to unearth. Their grasp could not hold forever.

At last one of the men turned his eyes toward the narrow path. Its Gatekeeper stood with tear filled eyes of expectation. The traveler called out asking, "What can we do? We heard the rumors of this land, and so we traveled long and far. But what can we do now to continue along the right path?"

The Gatekeeper looked him deep in the eyes. And smiled. He then responded by telling him that which His path had to offer. He spoke of the bread of life. He spoke of waters from which whoever drank would never thirst again. He spoke of eternal riches.

The words He spoke were so much sweeter than the deceitful gatekeeper and the treasures He offered so much greater that suddenly the wide path offered no lure at all. Its fleeting temptations were incomparable to the lasting pleasures of the narrow way. And so, one by one the men reached out toward the narrow Gatekeeper. One by one He took their hands and led them into His Father's land.

✝

If the first step toward true, Biblical holiness is an honest and candid look at our own sin then the second step lies in looking beyond it.

You see, believers often view Christianity as a choice contrary to pleasure. They believe that they can either live a life of gratification or a life of Christ. And so, pleasure and sin are often viewed as one in the same while God is viewed as some sort of killjoy who seeks to extract all gratification and pleasure from our lives.

These Christians have somehow forgotten that life's greatest pleasures are found in God, not apart from Him. They have somehow forgotten that the temptations of this world pale in comparison to the unfailing joy, emotional and spiritual fulfillment, peace of mind, sense of purpose, eternal certainty, soul quenching pleasure, and divine consolation that are found in Christian spirituality. As a result, they've become more concerned with repressing the desires of their flesh than with unleashing the actual desires of their heart.

But as we discussed in the last chapter, that viewpoint is a far cry from the true character of God. And as the previous parable illustrates, it is a far cry from the realities of our world.

God is not opposed to pleasure. God *created* pleasure. And so, true Christianity is not about resisting or denying pleasure. It's not about repression or suppression or oppression. In reality, Christian living is less about denying the wide path as it is about choosing the narrow path. It is less about resisting the lure of sin as it is about recognizing the lure of Christ.

"Turn your eyes upon Jesus,
Look full in His wonderful face,
And the things of earth will grow strangely dim,
In the light of His glory and grace."[144]

An Understanding or How to Properly Operate a Blender

Having said all of this, I am not pretending to offer some magical new two step program for overcoming temptation and compromise. I don't thing Christianity can be reduced to any kind of absolute formula.—Certainly not one with fewer steps than it takes to operate a blender.

What I'm actually talking about here is not so much a formula as it is an understanding. It is the same understanding Paul wrote about from prison when he said, "*Set your minds on things above, not on earthly things.*"[145] And again, while imprisoned under the emperor Nero, when he wrote, "*Flee the evil desires of youth, and pursue righteousness, faith, love and peace...*"[146]

This understanding is the only way you and I can avoid becoming a casualty of compromise. Without it we are left to struggle in our flesh, with our flesh. Resisting. Avoiding. Enduring. Attempting the impossible.

That's because trying to live an abundant, holy life in this hollow, fallen world is like trying to empty a fish bowl in the sea while swimming a mile below the surface. It's hopeless unless we replace the contents with something else entirely. Fill the bowl with rocks and it will drive out most of the water. Fill it with sand, even better. But trying to empty it without anything else to fill it with?—That's impossible.

Similarly, the only hope of purging ungodliness from our life is to replace it with something Godly. Romans 12:21 says, *"Do not be overcome by evil, but overcome evil with good."* And in the book of Matthew Jesus tells a parable saying, *"When an evil spirit comes out of a man, it goes through arid places seeking rest and does not find it. Then it says, 'I will return to the house I left.' when it arrives, it finds the house unoccupied, swept clean and put in order. Then it goes and takes with it seven other spirits more wicked than itself, and they go in and live there. And the final condition of that man is worse than the first."*[147]

In the end, you and I can never defeat compromise by starving the sin. We must first seek to feed the spirit. For we can never turn from our transgressions unless we first turn to our Lord.

Day Old Meatloaf

My friend Danny once witnessed a food fight in college. He claims he never threw a thing, yet he still walked away covered in spaghetti and ketchup and day old meatloaf.

If I may be honest with you one last time: *You and I are not like my friend Danny.*

Contemporary Christians often pass the guilt of sin unto this world in which we live. They mistake the pursuit of holiness for the pursuit of perfection. In the end, they fail to ever humble themselves by taking responsibility for their own actions.

But as we've discussed in this chapter, you and I are not innocent onlookers. In life, we are not blameless bystanders. We are not sitting on the sidelines watching some sort of eternal fight on pay-per-view. Rather, the fight is present and real in the heart of each of us.

For that reason we must learn to worry less about perfection and worry more about sincerity. We must become less troubled by the sin of society and become more troubled by our own. We must stop passing blame and start taking responsibility.

After all, the real problem is not this world.

The real problem is *me*.—That I know for sure.

The real problem is *you*.—Correct me if I'm wrong.

Chapter 4

Tolerance
Fundamentalism
Compromise
Materialism

Materialism

"People who want to get rich fall into temptation and a trap and into many foolish and harmful desires that plunge men into ruin and destruction. For the love of money is a root of all kinds of evil."[148]

—the Apostle Paul

"You know we are living in a material world
And I am a material girl."

—Madonna, "Material Girl"

"Golden shackles are far worse than iron ones."

—Mahatma Gandhi

The sun hung high above the lower Jordan Valley. The sand was so hot its heat pierced His thin, leather sandals. But Jesus continued. Laboring. Plodding.

His beard was matted with sand, His skin was chapped, and His eyes were dull. The robe nearly fell from His emaciated shoulders. But Jesus continued. Stumbling. Drudging.

It had been weeks since His last meal. Fasting in such heat was physically grueling and mentally testing. But that was the reason Jesus continued. That was the very reason He had come.

Then suddenly He looked up to see the hazy silhouette of a man standing in the far distance. Jesus stepped forward, squinting, hoping to better see the sudden stranger. But the man's face remained hidden. Despite the desert sun the man remained veiled in dark obscurity. It was as though he were a living shadow.

The stranger kept a silent distance between them. He remained at view's edge, watching, as if he were waiting for the precise moment to strike.

And then he did.

He was at Jesus' side in an instant, tempting Him with a sly, soothing tongue. His voice was strong. Not at all like Jesus felt. And his offer was enticing. But Jesus was able to withstand his lure.

So the shadowy stranger took Jesus to the temple pinnacle where he tempted Him again. His words played tricks on Jesus' mind. His cunning warped Jesus' reasoning. His temptations enticed Jesus' flesh. He was unrelenting. But again, Jesus was able to withstand.

Finally, the stranger took Jesus to a high cliff overlooking Jericho. From there they looked out onto the great cities of the world and all of their splendor. The stranger spoke again, his shadowy arm making a grand gesture from left to right. His voice was stronger than ever. Almost as if proud. Arrogant. *"All this I will give to you...."*

There was a long pause.

He allowed his words to permeate.

He allowed the offer to marinate.

Then he leaned closer and continued.

His voice was quieted now.

Almost a whisper, "*....if only you will bow down and worship me."* (Matt 4:1-11)

Ensnared by the Finite

It seems that little has changed in two thousand years. This world still showers us with splendor, but in the end it delivers only slavery. The enemy still promises pleasure, but in the end he delivers only pain.

There's always a catch. There's always a snare. Yet unlike Christ most of us are unable to resist the lure. Most of us, in fact, are more like raccoons...

†

A small box with a tiny hole and some bait is all that you need. No springs. No trap doors. Just a box, a hole, and some bait.

By placing the bait within the box a raccoon is lured to stretch its hand inside. Then, with food in hand the raccoon is unable to remove its paw from the box. The tiny hole which it had barely squeezed through before is much too small to allow a fist full of cuisine to pass back through. No matter how hard it tugs or twists the raccoon is trapped.

Unless, of course, it lets go of the bait.

I was amazed when I first learned how raccoon traps worked. I was amazed by their simplicity. I was amazed at how stubborn raccoons were and the way they refused to let go. But as amazing as it is, many of us are in the same sad scenario:

• The average American household has a credit card debt of *$8400*, with an average interest rate of 18.9 percent.[149]
—Yet we refuse to let go.

• In 2002 Americans paid a staggering *65 billion* toward credit card interest alone.[150] (That doesn't even include the interest on home mortgages, car loans and student loans.)
—Yet we refuse to let go.

• In 1970 Americans owed 5 billion in credit card debt. By 1997 that amount had sky rocketed to nearly *600 billion*.[151]
—Yet even still we refuse to let go.

Peter instructed us: *"Live as free men."*[152] His directive seems easy enough, but it has proven difficult. Paul also charged us, saying, *"You were bought at a price; do not become slaves of men."*[153] But we seem to have long forgotten our own worth. We seem to have neglected his warning.

As a result, many of us have become consumed by consumption and ensnared by the finite. Our priorities have become flipped upside down. Our values have become twisted beyond recognition.

Twisted Values (a.k.a. American Values)

Recently I read the words of Thomas Guthrie and I couldn't decide whether to laugh or cry. He writes: "If you find yourself loving any pleasure better than your prayers, any book better than the Bible, any house better than the house of God, any table better than the Lord's table, any persons better than Christ, any indulgence better than the hope of Heaven—take alarm."[154]

Take alarm?! Are you kidding me? The sirens in America have been blaring for so long that we have become deaf to them. His words are true, but seem a century past due.

God has given us His all. He "*so loved the world that He gave His only begotten son.*"[155] And He waits now, each and every day, with nail pierced hands of love and mercy to give you and me more than we could ever imagine. But often times we take what He offers and just throw it back in His face.

We pass up the infinite for the finite. We pass up the priceless for the worthless. We pass up the riches of heaven for the smut of this world.

In fact, a mere 12 percent of born-again adults tithe their income, and Christians spend seven times more on entertainment than they do on spiritual activities.[156] No wonder Jesus spoke more about money than about heaven or hell. No wonder there are 450 passages in the bible that deal with wealth. No wonder nearly one-fifth of Jesus' recorded words dealt with the issue of money, and nearly every time He taught on the issue He advised us to *give it away*.

"*Keep your lives free from the love of money and be content with what you have.*"[157]

"*Again I tell you, it is easier for a camel to go through the eye of a needle than for a rich man to enter the kingdom of God.*"[158]

"*If anyone has material possessions and sees his brother in need but has no pity on him, how can the love of God be in him?*"[159]

"*Whoever can be trusted with very little can also be trusted with much, and whoever is dishonest with very little will also be dishonest with much. So if you haven't been trustworthy in handling worldly wealth, who will trust you with true riches?*"[160]

"*If you want to be perfect, go, sell your possessions and give to the poor, and you will have treasure in heaven. Then, come, follow me.*"[161]

"*Some people, eager for money have wandered from the faith and pierced themselves with many griefs.*"[162]

BURIED ALIVE: A DISCUSSION ON OVERCOMING THE "SEVEN LIFELESS SINS"

"He who is kind to the poor lends to the poor."[163]

"It is for freedom that Christ has set us free. Stand firm, then, and do not let yourselves be burdened again by the yoke of slavery."[164]

✝

It's not that I think we're all selfish, greedy people. I don't think we're wicked. Rather, it's just that we've bought into the American lifestyle. We're lifeless.

We as Christians seek the same goals as the rest of society. We crave the same things. We gauge success by the same barometer. We horde. We indulge. We buy, buy, buy. As a result, we have somehow become numbed by America's standards of acquisition, and we've accepted its twisted value system.

I'm sorry, but I can't help but be bothered when I walk into many new churches today. As I walk past the Greek columns and chandeliers and people dressed to impress I can't help but wonder whether we're missing the point of what God's church is really supposed to be.

Just imagine if Jesus walked into your sanctuary on Sunday morning. Imagine if He walked up to the podium and cleared His throat to speak. Do you think He'd suggest you take up a special offering so that you can add on more square footage to your church building, with even more columns and chandeliers, facilities and amenities? Or do you think He would urge our hearts with tear filled eyes of love and mercy to reach out to our communities and to our world, working to help and to build His eternal kingdom rather than our own petty buildings?

The answer is obvious.

Now, imagine how all of this must look to an impoverished young boy from Zambia who lives off of less than $1 a day and who views America as a "Christian nation." He sees our lives of excess and extravagance. He watches day after day as we indulge in our material success. Does that image reflect the true teachings of Christ?

The answer is just as obvious.

Where is the servant hood? The generosity? The compassion? The kindness? The love? We often talk about our witness before unbelievers when it comes to things like sex and drugs, but what about our witness to this world when it comes to the way we prioritize and spend our money?

It seems that we are quick to call our country blessed. We are quick to thank God for all He's given us. Yet on the other hand we fail in realizing what difficulties, obligations and expectations come with such blessings. We fail in realizing how shameful our poor stewardship has become. We fail in realizing how immoral our materialism truly is.

> "John Stott once said our blindness to materialism is similar to the western culture's blindness to the sins of slavery in the eighteenth and nineteenth centuries. Today we look back in amazement that Christian people could not see it for the evil it was. And likely, thinks Stott, future generations, should they look back, will regard our day with the same perplexity: *How could they not have seen it?*"[165]

The Reality of Our Actions or If Kalinga Were Your Son

What we must realize is that that impoverished young boy from Zambia I mentioned earlier, who lives off of less than $1 a day, is not imaginary or theoretical. He is real. And his name is Kalinga.

You see, I met Kalinga in the rural village of Mopatizia, Zambia while doing missionary work there recently. One day as I was walking through the village he ran out to meet me. His ragged shirt was hanging loosely over his frail body and his skin was stretched tight over his thin bones, as he began to ask what life in America was like.

Kalinga and I started to walk and talk together, and as we did my heart started to break. I was troubled by the daily hardships he had to endure. I was embarrassed by the trivial troubles I'm so often consumed by. And I was ashamed by the fact that I wore a wardrobe worth more than the entirety of his possessions.

Kalinga met me everyday after that. We walked together, talking about hobbies and sports and girls and the differences between our two countries. By the end of my trip we had become true friends.

When it came time for me to return home Kalinga and I said our goodbyes. I knew then that I would never see him again. But I knew also that my life would never be the same because of him.

†

I tell you all of this to make a point. You see, it is easy for us as Christians to fall prey to passive ideology. As a result you and I talk as though the suffering in this world causes us to suffer. We talk as though it breaks our heart and that we want to make a difference. But in the end we often do little more than talk. We discuss in church what should be done and we theorize over cappuccino what could be done. Meanwhile *forty thousand* children die each and every *day* due to malnutrition.[166]

...Allow this reality to sink in for a moment...

America, a supposedly Christian nation, suffers from chronic obesity while millions of people around the world die from starvation. In fact, we constitute only 6 percent of the world's population yet we consume 43 percent of the world's resources.[167]

Scripture says, *"let us not love with words or tongue but with actions and in truth,"*[168] for *"the kingdom of God is not a matter of talk but of power."*[169] And in the book of James he asks: *"Suppose a brother or sister is without clothes and daily food. If one of you says to him, 'Go, I wish you well; keep warm and well fed,' but does nothing about his physical needs, what good is it? In the same way, faith by itself, if it is not accompanied by action is dead."*[170]

Yet despite what scripture says it seems that many Christians today have lost touch with the present and practical needs of this world. It seems we no longer know how to put our faith to work. As a result, children like Kalinga continue to die by the millions.

But you know what? If Kalinga were my son or your son I bet we would have stopped discussing the situation by now.

I bet we would have already shut our mouths, and done something about it.

A Street Corner Named Desire or What We are Worth

The other day I was flipping through a GQ magazine when Chase suddenly turned to me and asked, "Why do we even care?"

I tore my eyes from the new fall fashion page and answered his question with a look of confusion. "What are you talking about?"

"Luxury cars…Designer jeans…Big homes…Thin bodies…Any of it. All of it. Why do we care so much?"

I slowly nodded my head, pretending to ponder his question. But honestly I wasn't in the mood to think about it. So just as quickly as the moment emerged it quickly began to evaporate. Slowly our eyes and our desires were drawn back to the colorful pages laid out before us. We fell silent once again.

But later that night his words returned to me like rolling thunder. As I lay in bed I couldn't help but think about what he had said. I began to wonder why I was so obsessed with certain things; finite things like power, possession and prestige. Then I began to wonder whether these were my true desires at all.

Were these things what my heart truly longed for? Or, I wondered, were these things merely what I had been *told* to desire, what I had been *made* to desire?

> "American economist Thorsten Veblen uses the phrase 'conspicuous consumption' to suggest that certain items, including luxury automobiles, are often purchased more to make a statement as to who the owner thinks he or she is than to fulfill a need or even a *real* want. Christians, among with the rest of society, are being manipulated into gratifying *artificially* created wants while ignoring the basic needs…of the world."[171]

Like a broken television set, it seems that if you could cut to the heart of most Americans you would hear only fuzz. And you would see only a dull, lifeless stare. That's because most of us have for so long prostituted ourselves to the desires of this world that we no longer know what our own true desires even are!

Think about it. For many of you it may be the first time you ever have.

What do *you* want? Apart from what the world has told you, and despite what advertisers say, what do *you* desire? Is it a faster car and a bigger house? Or is it something *more*?

"Then you will know the truth, and the truth will set you free."[172]

"The Spirit of life set me free from the law of sin and death."[173]

BURIED ALIVE: A DISCUSSION ON OVERCOMING THE "SEVEN LIFELESS SINS"

"You have been set free from sin..."[174]

"So if the Son sets you free you will be free indeed."[175]

After that night with the GQ magazine I began to look at things differently. And I didn't like what I saw.

Television honors the world's richest men for their financial success. Fans worship celebrities for their beautiful bodies and glamorous lifestyles. Children idolize professional athletes for their abilities on the court. We don't seem to care if they have a string of broken families, and an absent spiritual life. As long as they are famous or have arrived financially we honor them, worship them, and idolize them.

In the meantime, no one seems to honor the men in the world who remain faithful to their wives, until death do they part. No one seems to worship the devoted mothers who successfully raise their children to be children of God. No one seems to idolize the children who resist peer pressure and stand strong for their convictions.

What is truly priceless in this world has become thought of as insignificant and even shameful, while what is actually insignificant and shameful has become thought of as priceless.

I wonder, why aren't charity workers treated like celebrities? Why don't we idolize men of faith and women of compassion? Seriously, just imagine a world with its priorities so accurate and true. In many ways it would be a world opposite of this one we live in today.

†

Henry Scoupal once stated, "The worth and excellency of a soul is to be measured by the object of its love." What you hold most dear in your life is a measure of the worth of your life. What you value most determines the value of your soul.

What does that say then about the soul of America when we value fame and fortune above all else? What does that say about you and me when our only measure of success is how much money someone makes?

As it turns out, financial wealth can truly make a man worthless. For when we relegate the value of Jesus Christ in our life we relegate the value of our own soul. And when we elevate the importance of this finite world we diminish our own importance.

But in truth you and I are worth more than a suit. We are worth more than the car we drive. We are worth more than the house we drive home to.

The advertisers may not want us to realize this, but God certainly does. In fact He once talked about what you and I are worth by saying, *"Are not two sparrows sold for a penny? Yet not one of them will fall to the ground apart from the will of your Father. And even the very hairs of your head are all numbered. So don't be afraid; you are worth more than many sparrows."*[176]

You see, we are worth more than all of this, unless this is all we choose to be worth.

Our Own Stupid Pocketbook

The company was downsizing. Within a week hundreds of employees suddenly found themselves unemployed. Among the hundreds were two men: Richard and James.

Richard was a good man. He was a hard worker and father of three. He had never shown much interest in God. But nonetheless, he had always been able to handle the ups and the downs of life. Always, until now.

James was a Christian. He was also a hard worker and had three children of his own. James had long ago given his life to God, and because of that commitment he too had been able to handle the ups and downs of life. Now was no exception.

Two weeks after being laid off Richard began to grow anxious. The pressure of unpaid bills was already piling high. The stress of an unknown future was already weighing on his shoulders.

James too was feeling the pressure. James too couldn't deny that there was a certain level of stress. But he remained faithful to God and certain of God's divine will.

Four weeks after being laid off Richard's anxiousness had grown into full fledged fear. What was going to happen? What was he going to do? They couldn't afford their current home on his wife's salary. Let alone the car or the boat or the vacation they'd planned. The financial strain had already taken a severe toll on his marriage. He and his wife were at odds. He snapped at his children for the slightest misstep. He had to find work soon.

James also began to consider his family's financial situation. They too couldn't afford to continue on his wife's salary. But James knew that cars and clothes were not the most important things in life. James knew that God was still in control, no matter how hot the fire of refinement might be. Now, in the midst of a financial crisis, was certainly not the time for him to push God aside and take the reigns himself. James remained faithful to God and certain of God's divine will.

Six weeks after being laid off Richard was angry. All that he had worked for was falling apart at the seams. All that he had achieved was becoming recent history. He found himself sleeping on the couch. His kids didn't want to be in the same room with him, and he couldn't blame them. He was slipping into depression.

James began to help around the house. Maybe it wasn't the most typical response to being laid off, but James sought to make the best of his situation. So, after job hunting each day he returned home and did household chores so that he could spend extra time with his wife and children in the evening. He still needed a job or otherwise they would have to move. Their future was still uncertain. His pride had still been shaken. But James remained faithful to God and certain of God's divine will.

Eight weeks after being laid off the company began hiring again. Within a week dozens of people were reemployed. Among the hired were two men: Richard and James.

†

Does true wealth have anything to do with money? Anything at all? Why then do we so often correlate the divine blessings of God with our own stupid pocket book?

In this simple story both Richard and James lost their jobs. They each endured uncertainty. They each faced financial despair. But they each perceived the situation in their own way, and they each handled the situation differently.

After two weeks Richard became anxious; James remained faithful. After four weeks Richard grew fearful and irritable; James continued to lean on the rock of Christ Jesus. After six weeks Richard become angry, on the verge of depression; James began to make the best of his situation, even still, remaining faithful that God was in control.

That is the abundant life Christ spoke of. Not assured employment and financial wealth, but so much more: joy and peace despite it all.

" for I have learned to be content whatever the circumstances."[177]

"I know what it is to be I need, and I know what it is to have plenty. I have learned the secret of being content in any and every situation, whether well fed or hungry, whether living in plenty or in want."[178]

"give me neither poverty nor riches, but give me only my daily bread. Otherwise, I may have too much and disown you and say, 'Who is the Lord?' Or I may become poor and steal, and so dishonor the name of my God."[179]

"godliness with contentment is great gain. For we brought nothing into the world, and we can take nothing out of it."[180]

You see, many of us have realized that possessions and prestige are hollow gods. So instead we've turned to Christ. But for what? Often times it is the "divine blessings" of (drum roll please): possessions and prestige! It seems that our values have become so twisted and our desires have become so blurred that even when we do look to the right place we still look for the wrong things.

But Jesus clearly said, *"A man's life does not consist in the abundance of his possessions."*[181] And Paul says they have been *"robbed of the truth…who think that godliness is a means to financial gain."*[182]

Despite what the world and even some churches may have you believe the real blessings of God are rarely measured in dollar signs. If they were then Pharaoh would have been the most righteous of his time and Mother Teresa the least of hers.

Christ spoke of love, charity, and sacrificial giving. He never spoke of economic benefits as a result of following Him. Such a "prosperity gospel" may sound good coming from the pulpit, but it flies in the face of the true teachings of Christ.

For in truth, God is not as interested in shaping your finances as He is in shaping *you*.

The Divine Paradox

It's sad that it seemingly needs to be said, but *Jesus did not die on the cross so that you and I may live affluent lives*. Rather, He died so that we may live life abundantly. And that abundance has little to do with worldly wealth.

BURIED ALIVE: A DISCUSSION ON OVERCOMING THE "SEVEN LIFELESS SINS"

This is true because you and I were made for more than this world has to offer. We were meant for more than the here and the now and the next 50 years. The Bible says that God *"has set eternity in the hearts of men,"*[183] and that *"our citizenship is in heaven."*[184] The Psalms declare that we are *"stranger[s] on earth,"*[185] and Peter pleaded with us *"as aliens and strangers in the world."*[186] And Jesus prayed for His followers, saying, *"They are not of the world, even as I am not of it."*[187]

For that reason this finite world can never reach the true depths of our souls. It can never sooth our fragile hearts. It can never satisfy our sincere desires. No matter how big the house or how foreign the car or how much stuff we acquire, by seeking contentment in the twisted values of this world we will only foster discontentment and greed.

Scripture says, *"Whoever loves money never has money enough; whoever loves wealth is never satisfied with his income."*[188] Like a drug, the more we get, the more we want. Like ocean water, the more we drink, the more we thirst. We are unhappy even if we get it.

And I walked earth's highway, grieving,
In my rags and poverty,
Till I heard His voice inviting,
"Lift your empty hands to Me!"

So I turned my hands toward heaven,
And He filled them with a store
Of His own transcendent riches
Till they could contain no more.

And at last I comprehended
With my stupid mind and dull,
That God could not pour His riches,
Into hands already full.[189]

Jesus once said that no one can serve two masters. The two are directly and proportionately related. *"Either he will hate the one and love the other, or he will be devoted to the one and despise the other. You cannot serve both God and money."*[190]

So, just as the raccoon must first let go of its enticement we must learn to let go of ours. We must let go of this world that we may embrace Jesus Christ. We must let go of the desires of our flesh that we may attain the true desires of our soul. We must let go of the finite that we may grasp the infinite.

That is the divine paradox, for to have more contentment in this world we must seek less contentment from this world.

"Seek first his kingdom and his righteousness, and all these things will be given to you as well."[191]

"Delight yourself in the Lord and he will give you the desires of your heart."[192]

"Why spend money on what is not bread, and your labor on what does not satisfy? Listen, listen to me, and eat what is good, and your soul will delight in the richest of fare."[193]

"Whoever trusts in his riches will fall, but the righteous will thrive like a green leaf."[194]

"Command those who are rich in this present world not to be arrogant nor to put their hope in wealth, which is so uncertain, but to put their hope in God, who richly provides us with everything for our enjoyment...so that they may take hold of the life that is truly life."[195]

Grasping the Infinite

The Zambezi River is some of the wildest white water in the world. It runs along the border of Zimbabwe, roaring through the rainforest with crocodiles slipping in and out of its waters. The stretch of it we'd set out to raft that afternoon had several class four and class five rapids. (The rating only goes as high as five.)

We each took our paddles and climbed inside the raft. I looked around at the other smiling faces and smiled in return. No one had any idea how close to death we were about to come...

We could hear the roar of the rapid before we could even see it. It sounded like a freight train rumbling through the jungle. It made the river sound as if it was alive and hungry and we were its prey.

Then, suddenly, we were upon it. We hardly had time to realize. Fear struck us as we began to paddle furiously. Fitfully. Futilely.

BURIED ALIVE: A DISCUSSION ON OVERCOMING THE "SEVEN LIFELESS SINS"

The water swallowed us whole. We sunk deep within roaring walls of water and then were spit back out again. The brutal strength of the current flipped over our entire raft. Bodies flew in every direction as the boat landed upside down. No one was able to remain inside as we were left to brave this class five rapid on our own.

Did I mention that there were crocodiles?

The rapid rolled me and spun me. Water rocked me from every direction. My lungs cried for air.

I no longer knew which way was up. I was struggling for my life, and the worst of it was that I knew I was struggling in vain. I was at the mercy of the Zambezi.

At that instant I thought that I was going to die.

It wasn't a mere consideration of what death may be like, it was the feeling that it had finally arrived. Not some time in the distant future. Not even some time in the near future. Now. It was all over. My chance had passed.

It's amazing how such a moment can help you to see the big picture of life.

✝

The bible says, *"death is the destiny of every man; the living should take this to heart."*[196] Be sure not to overlook the second half of that verse. We are not only destined for death, we are instructed to take this truth to heart.

We shouldn't be forced, like I was, to come face to face with our death before we evaluate our life. We must pause now to look at the whole picture, before the whole picture has passed us by.

"What is your life? You are a mist that appears for a little while and then vanishes."[197]

"For here we do not have an enduring city, but we are looking for the city that is to come."[198]

"Show, O Lord, my life's end and the number of my days; let me know how fleeting is my life."[199]

"This world in its present form is passing away."[200]

"our days on earth are but a shadow."[201]

"So we fix our eyes not on what is seen, but on what is unseen. For what is seen is temporary, but what is unseen is eternal."[202]

"The world and its desires pass away, but the man who does the will of God lives forever."[203]

I was reminded of this truth again when I recently attended a high school basketball tournament. I had returned to my home town for the holidays and went to the tournament with some of my old teammates. As we sit there among a sold out crowd we began to reminisce.

We talked about the big games we won and about the big games that got away. We talked about the good and the bad, the ups and the downs, the triumphs and the failures. As we talked I could almost feel the butterflies filling my stomach again. I could almost hear the crowd in my ears.

You see, in those years basketball was life. And life was basketball. We trained before school each morning. We practiced deep into the night each evening. We ate and we slept and we breathed basketball.

The reminiscing was fun, but then suddenly I realized how absurd it all had been. I thought to myself how ridiculous we'd all acted. I recognized—finally—how overly important the game had been to us at that age.

As this realization washing over my mind I looked out onto the basketball court. I looked into the faces of those young players, and as I did I recognized the same delusion in their eyes. Just as I had once been, they where absorbed with the moment and consumed by their juvenile dramas. They could not yet see how much things would soon change for them. They had no idea what was in store.

The importance of grades would soon give way to the importance of career. The dramas of girlfriends and boyfriends would some day give way to the dramas of marriage. Concerns of popularity and sports would eventually give way to the concerns of health, family, finance, and retirement.

Then they would see and realize what was truly important in life.

BURIED ALIVE: A DISCUSSION ON OVERCOMING THE "SEVEN LIFELESS SINS"

Then, I thought, they would see the bigger picture.

Or would they?

You see, we as adults are often just as blind as we were in our youth. We become consumed with issues and concerns which may be more impacting than popularity and sports, but they are just as finite. There is an even bigger picture to which we are still yet blind.

I believe that when we reach the end of this life and cross over into eternity we will look back on today much like I looked upon the basketball court that night. We will see millions of faces so consumed with trivial, finite matters that they are missing what truly matters. Rick Warren writes, "You will not be in Heaven two seconds before you cry out, 'Why did I place so much importance on things that were so temporary? What was I thinking? Why did I waste so much time, energy, and concern on what wasn't going to last?'"[204]

The point is not that our lives are short and insignificant. The point is that an eternity of infinite significance awaits us on the other side.

This is a precious realization that we as Christians must take to heart. For us to become truly free from the snares of this world we must first realize that which is infinitely beyond it. We must realize that as trivial as our adolescence seems in the light of here and now, the here and now will seem infinitely more trivial in the light of eternity.

Learning to Let Go

When I consider this world's needs in light of the way I spend money, and eternity in light of the way I live, I am ashamed. Very ashamed.

I claim to value life over possessions. I claim to care for the poor and misfortunate. But by the way I spend and live it seems I value everything from clothes to coffee over the true needs of others.

I could feed a child like Kalinga with the amount of money I used this morning in mouthwash. I could pay for his education with the money I spent for the shirt on my back. I could *change the course of his entire life* with little or no consequence to my own.

Maybe it is time I learned to let go.

Maybe it is time we all did.

For this reason I plea and pray that you and I will learn to release this finite world in which we live. I pray that we will let go of this world's lies and empty promises. I pray that we will let go of all the fleeting smut we've come to think is so precious.

For to be free we must first let go.

Afterthought: Ways to Let Go

Compassion International
1800-336-7676
www.compassion.com

World Vision
1800-434-4464
www.worldvision.com

Opportunity International
1800-793-9455
www.opportunity.org
getinfo@opportunity.org

Christian Children's Fund
1800-776-6767
www.christianchildrensfund.org

Habitat for Humanity
1800-422-4828
www.habitat.org
publicinfo@hfhi.org

Gospel for Asia
1800-946-2742
www.gfa.org

Data
www.data.org

Blood: Water Mission
www.bloodwatermission.org
info@bloodwatermission.com

National Coalition for the Homeless
202-737-6444
www.nationalhomeless.org

Chapter 5

Tolerance
Fundamentalism
Compromise
Materialism
Busyness

Busyness

"You are worried and upset about many things, but only one thing is needed."[205]

—Jesus of Nazareth

"It's been a hard day's night,
And I been working like a dog
It's been a hard day's night,
I should be sleeping like a log"

—The Beatles, "A Hard Day's Night"

"Our schedules get packed with the mundane and ordinary, and we become irritated with God when He interrupts us with the miraculous and extraordinary."

—Erwin Raphael McManus

He stumbled towards me clutching an old, rugged Elmo doll. His clothes didn't match and his shirt was on backwards, but he was smiling from ear to ear. Then suddenly his foot caught the edge of uneven concrete and he fell hard to the ground.

I rushed toward him and helped him to his feet. I looked at his face, expecting to see tears. But he was still smiling. Ear to ear. Pure joy.

You see, Trevor was not your average teenager. A severe mix of downs-syndrome and autism had left him completely non-verbal. From a distance he looked like any thirteen year-old, but inside his burly exterior was the fragile mind of a child.

As a volunteer at Camp Barnabas, a summer camp for children with disabilities, I would be responsible for helping Trevor. I would help him put on his socks and tie his shoes. I would help him find his way around camp and make sure he was on time. I would even cut his food and help him to eat.

I would help him. That is what I was there to do. I had no idea how much he would actually help me.

I picked up Trevor's Elmo doll and handed it back to him. He took it from me and patted it lightly on the head. Then he shuffled away. As I stood there watching him stagger down the path I was suddenly flooded with emotion. I thought of what his life must be like. I thought about all of the hardships he would endure. The ridicule. The stares.

With his mental disabilities I knew that he would never excel at academics or sports. He would never savor a poem by Emily Dickinson or delight in the art of Dechamp. He would never marry or have a family of his own.

It broke my heart. It seemed so unfair. I couldn't help but question why.

Why must Trevor live his entire life this way? Why would God allow something like this to happen to one of His children?

I closed my eyes and shook my head and tried to push the question to the back of my mind. I looked up to see Trevor further down the path, meeting and greeting everyone in sight. I ran to catch up, holding back the tears in my eyes.

For the most part that is how the rest of our week went. Trevor shuffled around camp meeting people—often for the third and fourth time—greeting each one with a smile and a hug. He showed each camper his precious Elmo doll, certain to never relinquish it. Meanwhile, I wrestled with a broken heart, wrestled with tears, and wrestled with the question why.

But then on the last night of camp, as I lay awake in bed, something happened that I cannot explain. I looked across the room at where Trevor was sleeping and suddenly, unexpectedly, I saw life through his eyes. It was so simple and clear and unmistakable, and finally I realized…

Trevor would face hardships in life, but the hardships he'd face were only physical. My struggles were much deeper. My limitations were much graver.

Trevor would face ridicule and stares. But he would return each scorn with a smile. He would view each stare through eyes of pure joy.

Trevor would never excel at sports or academics. He would never savor Dickenson or delight in Dechamp. And he would never have a family of his own. But Trevor excelled at hugs and smiles, laughter and joy. Trevor savored each moment with rich appreciation and he delighted in the simplicities of life as I never could. To Trevor everyone was family.

I closed my eyes and tucked my hands behind my head. I thought of Trevor's smile and in doing so couldn't help but smile silently to myself.

At that moment I could almost hear God saying, "That's why."

Someone Like Trevor

Trevor's priorities are clear. They are brilliantly simple. What matters most to Trevor is people and relationships, love and laughter. And to Trevor what matters most is all that matters.

He is not distracted by trends and fads. He is not ensnared by the rat race. He does not place people after possessions. He does not put tomorrow before today.

For this reason the world calls someone like Trevor handicapped. It labels him disabled and then shuffles him to the edge of society. But sometimes I wonder who it is that has the greater disability…

†

In today's world busyness is literally killing us. The majority of people say they are too busy and one third of Americans say they are "stressed out."[206] In fact, medical researchers estimate that stress contributes to 90% of all illnesses. And stress is related to the six leading causes of death in America: heart disease, cancer, lung ailments, accidents, cirrhosis of the liver, as well as suicide.[207]

…It seems to me that we could learn a lot from someone like Trevor.

†

In today's world we actually brag about being too busy. As if it were some kind of status symbol to be poorly prioritized and out of focus, we chat about how full our schedules are. We boast about how long it's been since we've had a day off or some time for ourselves. We discuss how little sleep we've gotten lately and how exhausted we are.

But God knows how important relaxation and prioritization is. He knows how susceptible you and I can be to busyness—So much so that one of His ten commandments is a Sabbath day rest.[208]

...It seems to me that we could learn a lot from someone like Trevor.

†

In today's world we don't even say hello with honesty. Instead we say things like, "Hey Bob. How's it going?" But we don't really mean it. Then someone like Bob responds, "Oh, pretty good. And you?" But he doesn't mean it either.

This truth is made obvious in the way that neither person even waits for a response to their own question. Instead, they offer hollow words and then hurry on with their day. It seems that we no longer have time for sincerity. We no longer have time for people and relationships. We no longer have time for the things that matter most.

Just imagine if we said what we really meant: "Hey Bob. I would ask you how you were doing, but honestly I don't care. And even if I did care I know that you wouldn't really take the time to tell me. So, instead I'll just nod and smile and keep on walking. That way we can save our precious time for things more important than friendship—Things like making money and spending money and..."

...No doubt about it, we could learn a lot from someone like Trevor.

A Loss of Direction

It is a delicate balance between busyness and laziness. (More on laziness in the next chapter.) Similar to the relationship of tolerance and fundamentalism, the high road is a narrow one with deep ditches on either side. Trevor seemed to understand this balance. But for most of us it is a narrow, slippery slope and if we drift too far either way we lose our direction.

That is exactly how I would describe myself at times when I've become encumbered by busyness—A loss of direction. I have never chosen busyness. I have never intended to push God to the end of the line. Yet somehow, somewhere along the way, He becomes entangled in a muddled mess of jumbled priorities and I tuck my soul away behind all of the errands and duties I have for the day, promising myself I will tend to it later when things at work are a little slower and things at home are a little calmer.

But you and I can not wait until our schedules are clear to follow Christ's teachings.

I believe it is one of the greatest lies we tell ourselves, that we will be different when the circumstances in our lives are different. We promise ourselves we'll be more generous with our money when we have more money to be generous with. We convince ourselves we'll be more dedicated to our spiritual lives when we finally find that perfect church family. We even justify our shameful actions by telling ourselves we'll be "better" when we're older and have less temptation to deal with.

But the simple truth is if you and I are not generous with our current salaries then we will not be generous with any salary. If you and I are not dedicated now, or if you and I are indulging sin now, then no outside circumstance will ever change that. Nothing will ever change unless we make a conscious and deliberate decision to change.

Similarly, if you suffer from busyness now you will always suffer from busyness. If you are too busy to spend quality time with your kids, to love your spouse, and to invest in lasting friendships then you will always be too busy. Unless you make a conscious change, your soul will forever remain tucked away in the folds of mundane busyness.

Plotting a Course

Exam Question #1. Please circle the best answer:
Johnny is at point A. He wishes to fly from point A to point B. Which direction should Johnny fly, and how long should he fly for?

A. He should fly due North for 3 hours.
B. He should fly due South for 12 hours.
C. He should fly due East for 7 hours
D. He should take a bus.

†

If you're confused by the previous question, then good…You're paying attention.

You see, we cannot possibly know which direction Johnny should fly when we have no idea where Johnny is. And we cannot possibly know how long he should fly for when we have no idea where he wants to go. In much the same way, you and I will never succeed in living these lives of ours to the full unless we know where we are and exactly where we want to be.

Scripture says to *"not be foolish, but to understand what the Lord's will is."*[209] Yet like a pilot taking off without ever plotting a course, many of us live our entire lives without ever examining the way we are living them. We never decide what we want for our lives. We never determine how we will achieve our aspirations. We never even consider what the Lord has in store. Then we look back years later and wonder why we never reached point B.

Ravi Zacharias comments on this reality by writing:

> "In the corporate world, every major company formulates a mission statement. That, in turn, is invoked when measuring achievements and failures. If a company does not know why it exists, then it will never know if it is failing or succeeding. How indicting, then, it is to all of us who will labor for hours to establish a mission statement for a company to sell toothpicks or tombstones but never pause long enough to write one out for our individual lives."[210]

Research has shown time and time again that people who make a tangible list of their goals are far more likely to reach those goals. This is true whether it is a to-do list for tomorrow or a mission statement for life. *"Therefore I do not run like a man running aimlessly; I do not fight like a man beating the air."*[211]

By clarifying your life's mission you will have a better understanding of what your own values and principles are. You will be better able to make decisions according to those values and principles. And you will become a proactive person, controlling the course of your life, rather than a reactive person who is controlled by the fickle winds and currents of this world.

BURIED ALIVE: A DISCUSSION ON OVERCOMING THE "SEVEN LIFELESS SINS"

"If the Lord delights in a man's way, He makes his steps firm."[212]

"Many are the plans in a man's heart, but it is the Lord's purpose that prevails."[213]

"Commit to the Lord whatever you do, and your plans will succeed."[214]

In the end we can all live the way we choose, as long as we take the time to choose the way we live.

For that reason I challenge you to write a mission statement for your own life. Consider what is important to you, what your values are, what excites you, what inspires you, what dreams and aspirations you have. Close your eyes and envision what life abundantly means to you. Pray for God's guidance and *"find out what pleases the Lord."*[215] Then write a mission statement for how you can make it a reality.

> Alice came to a fork in the road.
> "Which road do I take?" she asked.
> 'Where do you want to go?' responded the Cheshire cat.
> "I don't know," Alice answered.
> "Then,' said the cat, 'It doesn't matter."[216]

There is a space at the end of this chapter for you to use, or you can write your mission statement in a journal, the fold of your own Bible, et cetera. Write what you want, where you want. It doesn't matter. The only thing that matters is that you make it your own.

It can be a poem, a song, a series of bullet points, or even a sketch. It can be a wordy, rambling run on sentence like this one you are reading now that goes on and on talking about everything from work to family to watching television. It can be short and sweet.

There is no right or wrong answers. The possibilities are endless. There are no rules.

Well, except one: Don't bite off more than what you can chew.

What You Can Chew

When I was nine I had the worst Christmas of my life. It wasn't the year I discovered Santa Claus was some sort of heartless hoax perpetrated by adults on their innocent, trusting children. It wasn't even the year I found my stocking filled with coal.

In fact, I had known mom and dad were the real Santas of our family for quite some time. And as for presents, my bedroom floor was practically covered with Transformers and G. I. Joes. No coal in sight.

What nearly ruined my Christmas was an ordinary looking white envelope. This particular Christmas I had apparently reached some sort of echelon in life where I was not only given presents but was also entrusted with my own money for the after Christmas sales. At the beginning I was thrilled. Ecstatic. What was I going to buy first? Endless possibilities danced through my head.

But then it happened. The source of my joy suddenly became the root of my misery.

As my sister flipped through the television channels she paused on a local telethon. I stood there, a nine year old boy with a wad of cash in my hand as images of starving children flickered across the screen.

For the first time in my life I didn't want any more toys.

I remember looking down at the white envelope and my white knuckles clutching it. And I remember the tug at my heart to give it away. A local charity, a foreign charity, it didn't matter. At that moment I didn't care. I just had to do something generous with my money. Something charitable. Something of value.

But then just as quickly as the desire arose within me to give my money away, the desire arose within me to keep it. I may have had all I needed, but I certainly didn't have all I wanted. After all, what difference would my donation really make?

Greed stood on one shoulder like one of those little, red pitch-forked devils you see in sitcoms. He dangled a dozen toys in front of me, tempting me to keep the money for myself. Complete selflessness stood on the other shoulder like a tiny angel. It had two feathery wings, a white robe and a hallow.

But it didn't have any toys.

I struggled deep into the night, combating between these too desires. I didn't know what to do. It was a battle of epic proportions. But then suddenly I realized something. After hours of torment the truth finally dawned on me:

BURIED ALIVE: A DISCUSSION ON OVERCOMING THE "SEVEN LIFELESS SINS"

I had become so preoccupied with the thought and ensuing struggle of giving *all* my money away that I'd never even considered giving a proper portion.

†

You see, God doesn't ask us to give all we have or to live in complete poverty. But the enemy had tried to dangle such an unachievable vision before me that I nearly failed to attempt the achievable. He had tried to get me to bite off more than I could chew.

That, I think, is one of his most common strategies. Not just with money, but with goals, aspirations, and even daily responsibility. He shows us what all we cannot do in hopes that we never attempt what we can.

But when asked how we could possibly feed the billion starving children in the world Mother Teresa once responded, "One at a time." As it turns out, that is the only way to truly make a difference. And that is the only way to truly live our lives.

> If I can stop one heart from breaking,
> I shall not live in vain:
> If I can ease one life the aching,
> Or cool one pain,
> Or help one fainting robin
> Unto his nest again,
> I shall not live in vain.[217]

Instead of becoming overwhelmed by the pain and suffering that's beyond our control we must start causing all of the joy and happiness that is within it. As Christians we must focus less on what others aren't doing and make sure that we are. In the end we must move beyond what we cannot do by doing what we can.

†

Thomas Carlyle once said, "Our main business is not to see what lies dimly at a distance, but to do what lies clearly at hand." And the apostle Paul wrote, *"Do not be anxious about anything, but in everything, by prayer and petition, with thanksgiving, present your requests to God."*[218]

For these reasons you and I should not allow the stress and strain and vastness of life to take our focus off of what matters most in it.

After all, if you think about it, life is a lot like finding the bathroom in the middle of the night. Sometimes the hallway is pitch-dark. You are unable to see your hand in front of you. But if you take it one step at a time, moving steadily toward that bright sliver of light along the door's edge, sooner or later you're destined to make it. It's a much better solution than running frantically through the night or trying to make the entire distance with one blind leap.

In the same way, we can overwhelm ourselves with obligations and expectations. We can plan, stress and fret. We can weave ourselves into a ball of anxiety, and then spread ourselves as thin as a dime left on the railroad tracks.

Or we can take one step at a time.

One day.

One hour.

One minute.

One moment.

One task.

We can do what we can, and then leave the rest to God. If we do then in the end we will be more positive and productive than a life of busyness could ever offer. And we'll certainly enjoy life more along the way.

"Take My yoke upon you and learn from Me, for I am gentle and humble in heart, and you will find rest for your souls. For My yoke is easy and My burden is light."[219]

"Who of you by worrying can add a single hour to his life? Since you cannot do this very little thing, why do you worry about the rest?"[220]

"Do not let your hearts be troubled. Trust in God; trust also in Me."[221]

"Consider how the lilies grow. They do not labor or spin. Yet I tell you not even Solomon in all his splendor was dressed like one of these. If that is how God clothes the grass of the field, which is here today, and tomorrow is thrown into the fire, how much more will He clothe you…"[222]

BURIED ALIVE: A DISCUSSION ON OVERCOMING THE
"SEVEN LIFELESS SINS"

To Enjoy Life

I recently watched an interview on television with one of the most successful business men in America. During his life he had amassed billions of dollars. He owned hotels and casinos and cars and boats and houses. Sure he had left behind a dozen broken families in the wake, but nonetheless, he was an enormous success by the world's standards.

I sat there watching this successful billionaire as he began dispensing advice on how I too could be a billionaire:

First, he said to never take a vacation.

Second, he said to sleep less.

Third, he said…

…I turned him off, called my travel agent, and went to bed.

✝

If you crave cars and houses above all else in life, then that man's advice may be exactly what you're looking for. If you prioritize prestige and wealth over people and relationships, then by all means work more and sleep less. But that's not what I wrote as *my* mission statement. That's not what *I* want out of life.

Scripture says *"Do not wear yourself out to get rich; have the wisdom to show restraint."*[223] For that reason I had rather enjoy my life than work it away. I had rather spend time with my friends than with my job. I had rather look at my fiancée than at a computer screen.

I think that most people would agree. Yet by the way we live our lives it seems that we have become more focused on the things of life than on life itself. We have become so overwhelmed with living that we've forgotten how to *live*.

Perhaps we need a reminder…

33 Ways to Enjoy Life

1. Always, always, always put first the things that matter most.
2. Love your spouse and family unconditionally.
3. Show it.
4. Find a hobby that you really enjoy.
5. Actually honor the Sabbath.
6. Get a pet.
7. Always give people the benefit of the doubt.
8. Take dance lessons or join a bowling league.
9. Believe in something worth believing in.
10. Attempt the impossible.
11. Dream.
12. Start a weekly book or movie club.
13. Take a trip somewhere that doesn't speak English.
14. Say hello and mean it.
15. Keep in touch with old friends.
16. Create new family traditions.
17. Watch television for 30 minutes to an hour each day. No more. No less.
18. Look them in the eye and say "I love you."
19. Don't interrupt others.
20. Listen.
21. Listen more.
22. When in doubt, always ask yourself whether it will matter five years down the road.
23. As important as it is to have a life goal never forget to enjoy the present.
24. Spend a moment with the Lord each morning before you get out of bed.
25. Get plenty of fresh air.
26. Always get a good night's sleep.
27. Keep things simple.
28. Worry less about what you are "supposed" to do.
29. Worry even less about what others think.
30. Read a fiction book you've always wanted to read.
31. Challenge yourself by seeking out perspectives very different than your own.
32. Instead of surrendering happiness to make more money, surrender money to make someone more happy.
33. Instead of living by this world's standards, live according to your own mission statement.

BURIED ALIVE: A DISCUSSION ON OVERCOMING THE
"SEVEN LIFELESS SINS"

Number 34

If I could add one more thing to that list it would be for each of us to find a solitary place of our own; a place where we could go each morning to be alone with ourselves, our thoughts, and our Lord; a place where we can breathe deeply of life and truth and self reflection.

Perhaps you have a separate room in your house that you can withdraw to, or better yet, an outside space of your own. Perhaps you can rise early in the morning before anyone else is awake. No matter where or when you do it just be sure to have a comfy chair to sink into and meditate.

I use the word meditate because that's exactly what is missing from the lives of many Christians today. We may have our daily quiet time where we read a scripture and say a prayer, yet without a meditative mindset it often becomes a time of obligation and duty where we spend forty seconds reading a passage of Scripture and then we check God off our list of things to do for the day. But that is not what our relationship with God is supposed to be like. Such a quiet time only feeds our hectic, busy lifestyles.

In truth, our Lord is not something to be checked off a list. He is Someone to be experienced. Known. Savored.

And our spiritual lives are not something to be done. They are who we are.

"Very early in the morning, while it was still dark, Jesus got up, left the house and went off to a solitary place, where He prayed."[224]

"When Jesus heard what had happened, He withdrew by boat privately to a solitary place."[225]

"At daybreak Jesus went out to a solitary place. The people were looking for Him and when they came to where He was, they tried to keep Him from leaving them."[226]

"Then, because so many people were coming and going that they did not even have a chance to eat, He said to them, "Come with Me by yourselves to a quiet place and get some rest." So they went away by themselves in a boat to a solitary place."[227]

Don't get me wrong, reading a passage of Scripture and saying a prayer is a great way to meet our Lord. It's just that it's not the only way. And for many of us it's not the best way, whether we realize it or not.

I fear that there are thousands of people in America who have been told how to spend their time with God, as if it where specifically outlined in the Bible and there was no other way to do it. Consequently, these people have been trying to live a spiritual life that was never intended for them.

Like putting on a shirt backwards, they could tell from the beginning that something wasn't right. They knew in their hearts that something was wrong. But they were told that if they'd only try harder they would benefit from it. If they would only become better Christians, more regimented and disciplined, then in time the shirt would fit.

But I don't think that describes a healthy relationship with God. I don't think that is how He intended it. In truth, I think that your spiritual journey should be less about making someone else's method fit and more about finding your own.

So, tomorrow morning get a hot cup of coffee, a journal, a good book, your Bible, and your favorite CD. Stretch. Then sit back and follow your heart with honesty.

Read what you want. Write what's on your mind. Share with God what's in your heart. Dance if the urge stirs you.

This time is your time with God, your time to connect. So do it in whatever way your heart leads. Do whatever your soul desires. The most important thing, of course, is that you do it.

Things that Matter, Things that Last

A recent survey done by Cynthia Langham at the University of Detroit found that parents and children spend less than 14.5 minutes a day talking to one other.[228] When you compare that number to the amount of time we spend with our daily commute it is hard to tell where our true priorities are. — Or perhaps it is terribly easy.

Another survey, this one done by Dr. Urie Bronfenbrenner, polled middle-class fathers to determine how much time they spent each day with their one-year-old kids. Their responses concurred with Langham's survey, averaging between fifteen and twenty minutes. However, when Dr. Bronfenbrenner attached microphones to the children to record the amount of time they actually interacted with their fathers they found the average time to be a mere *37 seconds!*[229]

†

As I read statistics like these I am reminded of how hard it is to avoid busyness, how hard it is to keep life prioritized, and how hard it is to keep things in proper perspective. For some reason it is so much easier to be bombarded by busyness. It is easier to forget what matters most and to get caught up in the things that don't. It is easier to live lifelessly.

That is why I've recently decided to be less serious about unimportant things. I don't care anymore if someone cuts in front of me in line. I don't care anymore if Brecca gets crumbs in the car seat. I don't even care if we have the smallest house on the block.

Instead I've decided to get more serious about the things that matter most. I'm going to get more serious about having fun. I'm going to get more serious about friendships and laughter. I'm going to get more serious about love.

After all, I doubt that any of us will write about big houses or crumbless car seats in our personal mission statements. Rather, we'll most likely write about family and friends, love and relationships.—Things that matter, things that last. How sad it is, then, that those are the very things we often push to the end of the line.

In truth, I think it's time we all got more serious about the things that matter and less serious about the things that don't. I think it's time we entrusted our busy lives to the peaceful hands of God. And I think it's time we started enjoying this beautifully ridiculous thing that we call life.

I know Trevor would agree.

My Personal Mission Statement:

Afterthought: 33 More Ways to Enjoy Life

35. Don't ever be too prideful or too stupid to ask for help.
36. Make it a point to eat dinner as a family.
37. Get in the habit of buying new music every so often.
38. Get out of the habit of criticizing others.
39. Make a list of all the things you've always wanted to do around the town you live, and then start doing them.
40. Let your answering machine get it.
41. Sponsor a child.
42. Buy some massage oil.
43. Be an organ donor.
44. Go out on dates with your spouse.
45. Never stop learning.
46. Keep a journal.
47. Admit when you're wrong.
48. Become genuinely interested in the lives of others.
49. Learn to see the bit of truth in opinions you disagree with.
50. Whenever you can, pull some strings to help someone else.
51. Worry less about politics; that's all it is anyway.
52. Take more pictures.
53. Be more thankful.
54. Make your home an open invitation.
55. Make a deal with your spouse to spend less than $15 on Christmas presents for each other this year.
56. Play.
57. Pray.
58. Live below your means.
59. Avoid clutter.
60. Use your fireplace.
61. When the sky is clear and the stars are out, look up.
62. Enjoy the outdoors more.
63. Be more flexible.
64. Drink more water.
65. Eat more healthy.
66. Take a moment to consider what you enjoy most in life
67. Start enjoying it more.

Chapter 6

Tolerance
Fundamentalism
Compromise
Materialism
Busyness
Laziness

Laziness

"From Him the whole body…grows and builds itself up in love, as each part does its work."[230]

—the Apostle Paul

"I don't want to work
I want to bang on the drum all day.
I don't want to play
I just want to bang on the drum all day."
—Todd Rundgren, 'Bang on the Drum All Day'

"Dream as if you'll live forever. Live as if you'll die today."
—James Dean

So there I was, lying in bed, praying to God for the desire to read. It may seem a bit odd. It sure seemed odd to me. But let me back up and explain and then maybe it will make a little more sense…

I was a sophomore in college at time and up until that point in my life I had never read a book. I had begun a few, but I'd never finished a single one. Then I spent a month in China where I made a friend who had a passion for reading.

When we talked he would share lesson after lesson that he'd learned from ancient philosophers and classic theologians. When we would discuss issues he would always draw upon this wealth of wisdom and understanding. It was clear to me that reading was a passion of his. It was also clear that this passion had had a very real and positive impact on his life. And so, to put it plainly, I was jealous.

I wanted what he had. I wanted to know how he'd developed such a discipline in his life. I wanted to know how I could develop such a discipline in my own.

Then he surprised me by telling me his story. He said that he used to loathe reading. He, just like me, had rarely begun a book and even more rarely had finished one. It wasn't that he didn't want to, but every time he began the desire would flee like a crook in the night.

He wanted to read, yet he hated to. He knew he should, but he just couldn't. The spirit was willing, but the body was weak.

He was speaking my language.

So one day he said that he prayed to God for the desire to read. He actually prayed that God would swell a desire within him that would overcome his short attention span and simple laziness. And so, just a short time later he had cultivated a healthy appetite for books. He was a changed man.

Honestly, I didn't quite know what to think. I mean, I had heard of answered prayer, but could God really influence my desires? Did He care enough about me to intervene in my reading habits?

Nonetheless, when I returned from China I had a new resolve to read, and a new game plan to make it happen. —Which brings us back to where my story began, lying in bed, praying to God for the desire to read.

I didn't really know what to say. I think Jesus forgot to mention this part when he taught his disciples how to pray. So I just spoke from the heart. I asked God to work in my life, increasing my desire to read so that I may grow in Him. Then I sat back and awaited my miracle.

But nothing happened.

At all.

I had prayed to God for a desire to read, but He hadn't seemed to notice.

A month passed and I still hadn't read a word. Two months passed. Nothing. Three months passed. Still nothing.

After four months I had given up all hope and nearly forgotten about the whole silly ordeal when I finally comprehended something. Despite all of my prayer, hope, confusion and frustration I finally realized that *I didn't even have a book!*

What did I expect, for God to give me the desire to read and then to drop the book in my lap?

I had prayed for the desire, but I'd done nothing about it. I had prayed for God's divine intervention, but I'd failed to stop by my local Barnes & Nobles. I hadn't met my end of the bargain.

Not that buying a book was a big risk or a huge step of faith. Luckily for me, in this case God didn't demand either. He demanded only that I do *something*.

Faith, Grace & A Little Work or A Prayer of Procrastination

Reading is now one of my favorite things in this world. And as I look back it's clear to see that my prayers were answered after all. They just weren't answered in the exact way I thought they would be.

They never are.

Instead, God wanted me to do something. He wanted me to act. He wanted me to roll up my sleeves and do a little work.

He always does.

You see, unbelievers often look for answers in their own way, through their own efforts. They labor deep into the night thinking that if they could only work a little harder they could fix the problems and right the wrongs. They visit counselors and therapists and even psychics. They work in the flesh, but never consider the spirit. They never consider turning to God.

Christians often do the opposite. To a fault.

We pray for God's help and guidance. We pray for His divine intervention with a problem we face or an ambition we have. But then often times we do nothing about it.

We pray that He will heal a wounded relationship, yet we continue to hold a grudge. We pray that He will help us to overcome a destructive addiction, yet we never seek support. We pray that He will use us to spread His love and eternal truth, yet we refuse to live the kind of life He uses.

Like me in my pursuit of reading, we somehow expect God to work a miracle in our life and then to drop a book in our lap. But we cannot live lifelessly and then expect God to grant us life abundantly. After all, true discipleship is defined by what we *do*, not by what we say.[231]

✝

One of the laziest habits I have is to ask someone if they need help. It may sound like I am being helpful, but in honesty I am only trying to *appear* helpful.

When I see my fiancée Brecca cooking I'll ask, oh so sweetly, "Honey, is there anything I can do?" And when I see a friend struggling to carry boxes down the hall I'll speak up like some sort of selfless hero, "Hey buddy, if you need anything just let me know."

But if I really meant it I wouldn't inquire whether or not I could help. I would just help. I wouldn't ask. I would act.

If I really meant it I wouldn't ask God so often either.

What I'm talking about are those questions we already know the answers to. When it comes to charity, for instance, we know that we should be generous givers. When it comes to our faith we know that we should be active. And when it comes to risk taking we know that we should trust God in whatever direction He is pulling us.

We don't need permission to do what the Bible has already commissioned. We don't need to ask when the answer has already been given.

Yet when our heart compels us to act we often quiet it by promising to pray for the answer. At times like this we aren't using prayer to seek truth. We are only using prayer to delay, hoping in time that the yearning will fade.

Erwin Raphael McManus writes about this, saying:

> "I cannot count the number of times I have given counsel to individuals who seemed unable to discern what was the right thing to do. You would think those situations were highly complex and difficult to unravel, yet most of the time the counsel I gave was not the result of high discernment or unique intuition. Their situation was so clearly defined in the Scriptures that there was no ambiguity about what they should do. Too often the response was the same: 'I need to pray about it.'"[232]

After all, I didn't pray about it before I last decided to eat at a restaurant. I certainly didn't pray about it before I signed up for cable. And the last time Brecca and I saw something at the mall we liked we didn't leave it for later, telling ourselves, "We need to pray about this."

Why then do we so often insist on prayer when it comes to working and serving and helping others?

Don't misunderstand me, prayer is vital. I doubt that any of us will ever comprehend the depth and power of communing with our Lord. And of course we must always wait patiently for God's guidance, rather than acting hastily on our own. But at the same time we must stop kidding ourselves, pretending to seek the will of God when we are actually avoiding it. We must stop using prayer as a lifeless tool of procrastination.

†

The book of Ephesians says that *"it is by grace you have been saved, through faith…not by works, so that no one can boast."*[233] However, we mustn't miss the very next verse. It continues by saying, *"For we are God's workmanship, created in Christ Jesus to do good works."*[234]

You see, as Christians we are saved by faith. But to be saved by faith means we are to be workmen of Christ. — Workmen, not for our deliverance, but *because* of our deliverance. — Workmen, not because we have to, but because we *desire* to. For work has nothing to do with eternal salvation. Yet according to scripture it has everything to do with life abundantly.

For this reason you and I must find the balance between grace and works, laziness and busyness, love and labor. We must ask less and act more. We must rise above the lifelessness of lethargic Christianity. — Even if that means opening a few car doors.

Opening Car Doors or Love Made Visible

The sign on the door read:

Members only

No girlz allowed

Bobby knocked hesitantly. This was his first time to ever visit the Rag Tag Clan's secret club house. He had heard rumors of what the inside looked like and had heard tales of their legendary pranks. But he was not a member. In fact, he was the only boy in the neighborhood who wasn't.

He knocked again. The door cracked. Johnny from two blocks down peered out at him with one eye. "What's the secret knock?" he asked.

"I don't know," Bobby said, "But I want to find out. I want to become a member."

Johnny's eye narrowed. He looked Bobby up and down, grunted, and slammed the door shut again.

Bobby's face sank. His hope and excitement began to evaporate, replaced by embarrassment and shame. He glanced at his watch. It was almost time for dinner. His mom would be calling for him soon. Maybe he should come back tomorrow. Maybe he was better off not being a member anyway. Maybe he should start his own secret club…

Suddenly the door swung open. Johnny stood with a wide smile, surrounded by every boy in the neighborhood. He gestured Bobby in.

Inside, the walls were formed by a patchwork of scrap wood and cardboard. A bright blue tarp draped lazily overhead. A dozen scattered milk crates served as chairs, and stacked wooden palettes formed a stage against the far end. It was small and cramped, swaying with each gust of wind, but to Bobby the place felt like a palace.

He was ushered to the front. Johnny stood at his side and quieted the crowd to speak. "Rag Tags, I'm proud to announce that we have a new candidate for membership." The crowd erupted in cheers. They all began to strike their milk crates with sticks and chant their approval. All, except for one.

Roger was the neighborhood bully. He lived only three houses down from Bobby and they had never gotten along. He stood in the back with his arms crossed, a scowl written across his face.

Johnny continued, "But as we all know, any candidate must first prove themselves worthy to be a Rag Tag. Are there any suggestions?" A murmur immediately engulfed the clubhouse. The room became filled with mischievous laughs and wide eyes of wonder.

Bobby overheard someone mention toilet papering the old lady's house on the corner. Someone else discussed things he could stuff into mailboxes. Then suddenly Roger spoke. His voice was loud and demanding. Everyone became silent and turned toward the back to listen.

BURIED ALIVE: A DISCUSSION ON OVERCOMING THE "SEVEN LIFELESS SINS"

"I think that if ol' Bobby here wants to be a Rag Tag he should have to *find out*." A slight grin broke the scowl on one side of his face as Roger sit back down and crossed his arms again.

No one spoke a word. Mouths hung open, as the entire clubhouse sit motionless. Bobby couldn't tell if they were amazed, confused, scared, or all of the above.

But what did Roger mean? *Find out?* Find out *what?*

He turned to Johnny for answers. But Johnny looked just as dazed as the others. Finally Bobby broke the silence. "What's Roger talking about? What do I have to find out before I can be a member?"

Johnny turned to face him, his eyes still dancing around the room. Then he placed his hand on Bobby's shoulder and took a deep breath to speak. He looked him in the eyes as if he were about to tell him his dog had died. Then he said, "Bobby, he's talking about love."

Johnny swallowed hard and continued, "You see, we have lost five members this year. Three the year before. We need to know why." He took his hand from Bobby's shoulder and leaned closer, "When we asked them why they were leaving they all said it was because they were in love with a girl."

He said the words as if they were forbidden, and Bobby knew why. Girls were disgusting. They didn't know how to play. They could never keep secrets. And they were never dirty enough.

"We want you in our club, Bobby. But before we can let you, you must find out for us. Find out what they mean when they say that they are in love. Find out the meaning of this word."

Bobby looked out at the other members. They sit on the edge of their milk crates waiting for his response. What would he do? He had no idea what it meant to be in love and he had no idea how he would find out. But this was his only chance to be a member. And so, he took a deep breath and scanned the audience until he found Roger. He looked him in the eyes and then declared, "I'll do it."

His words brought the house down.

Bobby ran toward the door in excitement. The boys parted for him like the Red Sea. Once he was outside he climbed onto his bike and bolted toward town. But as the sound of cheering faded so did Bobby's confidence. How was he going to find out? How was he going to learn the meaning of love?

Then Bobby got a brilliant idea. He biked to an expensive restaurant along the riverfront. It served fancy dishes and had a name Bobby couldn't pronounce. He had heard that this made it romantic, so he parked his bike and hid in a bush, waiting for couples to emerge.

Within a few minutes a couple exited the restaurant. Bobby peered across the parking lot and watched their every move. But Bobby could clearly see that this couple was not in love. They were cold and distant as they walked to their car in silence. They climbed in and drove away.

Bobby shook his head in disappointment. Perhaps his plan wouldn't work after all.

But then suddenly a second couple emerged. In contrast to the first couple, they clearly loved one another. They were cheerful and talkative. They were full of smiles and laughter. They sauntered through the parking lot, and when they neared their car the man ran ahead to open the car door for his date. He then walked around, climbed into his own seat and drove away.

Bobby smiled with the satisfaction of knowing what love meant. He jumped to his feet and ran to his bike. He climbed on and began to peddle frantically back to the secret clubhouse.

He arrived just before sun down, hoping that someone would still be there. He banged on the door, nearly knocking it from its hinges. It swung open and he was gestured in again. He tore through the crowd and took the stage beside Johnny, who stood amazed he'd returned so soon.

Bobby couldn't contain his excitement. He stood grinning ear to ear. The others couldn't contain their eagerness. They began striking their milk crates with sticks and calling out for the answer.

Bobby puffed out his chest and cleared his throat. He raised his hand to quiet the audience. Then he affirmed, "To be in love means that you open car doors for one another."

He was declared a Rag Tag on the spot.

†

Of course love is more complicated than opening car doors. Bobby and his Rag Tag friends certainly did not grasp the infinite complexities of love and devotion. Yet in its simplest form they seemed to have had a perfect understanding of what true love is.

Love is selfless. It is unconditional. It is doing for another, not because you must but because you want to. It is working out of desire rather than out of obligation.

In the same way, in its simplest form, that's also what it means to love Christ Jesus. That is what Kahlil Gibran meant when he said,

BURIED ALIVE: A DISCUSSION ON OVERCOMING THE "SEVEN LIFELESS SINS"

"Work is love made visible." That is what James meant when he said, *"faith without deeds is dead.*[235]*"* And that is what God meant when He said, *"If you love me, you will obey what I command.*[236]

> "I cannot work my soul to save,
> For that my Lord hath done;
> But I will work like any slave,
> For the love of God's dear Son."[237]

Without this love from Christ, for Christ, we will never overcome our lazy, lifeless sin nature. If we try we will only fail, and at best we will become cold and legalistic Christians. Donald Miller writes about this saying:

> "Our 'behavior' will not be changed long with self-discipline, but fall in love and a human will accomplish what he never thought possible. The laziest of men will swim the English channel to win his woman. I think…that by accepting God's love for us, we fall in love with Him, and only then do we have the fuel we need to obey."[238]

You see, grace and works are often understood as being contrary to one another, like two forces pulling at our soul in opposite directions. Yet as it turns out they are not contrary, but rather complimentary. Like a swelling storm they actually build and perpetuate one another.

And so, only by accepting and reciprocating the love Christ offers us will we ever be able to obey the commands He gives us. And only by obeying His commandments will we be able to accept and return His love.

For this reason you and I should work to grow in Christ. We should work to seek truth, insight and understanding. We should work to love one another. We should work in Him, allowing Him to work through us.

And we should not delay a moment longer…

Some Sort of Miraculous Bank Account

Imagine for a moment that you have some sort of miraculous bank account that is automatically credited $1440 dollars a day. The only catch is that whatever money you don't spend is erased from your account each midnight. No saving. Each morning you wake with $1440 dollars, no more, no less, and whatever you don't spend is lost forever. What are you going to do?

Hmmm...

How about: Spend! Spend! Spend!

You'll buy all the things you ever wanted. Or else you'll give it all away. One way or another, you'll be certain not to waste a penny. Right?

Why then don't we treat our lives with the same urgency and worth as we do our money?

You see, there are 1440 seconds in every day. Whatever time we don't use is erased each midnight. No saving. Each morning we wake with 1440 seconds, no more, no less, and what ever we don't spend is lost forever. Yet by the way many of us are living, it seems that we are more concerned with wasting wealth than we are with wasting *life*.

†

This is a simple illustration that was told to me years ago, but ever since then it has had a profound impact on the way I strive to live. Notice that I said the way I *try* to live. No doubt about it, my life at times still wastes away to this thing called lifelessness. But on those days and at those moments this illustration calls out like a siren, prompting me to make the most of my life. It beckons me to live each day, and it reminds me of the words once written by John Greenleaf Whittier:

For all sad words
of tongue or pen
the saddest are these;
It might have been!

Truthfully, I don't think there's anything sadder than a wasted life. There is nothing more heartbreaking than being buried alive. Scripture seems to agree. It tells us that we should *"be very careful, then, how [we] live—not as unwise but as wise."* And the way to do that it says is *"by making the most of every opportunity."*[239]

Even so, many Christians today seem to be satisfied with the expectation of heaven. As a result, they seem to completely overlook abundant life here on earth. They have settled for salvation in Christ when, believe it or not, He has offered us more. In his book *The Divine Conspiracy* Dallas Willard comments on this by writing:

BURIED ALIVE: A DISCUSSION ON OVERCOMING THE
"SEVEN LIFELESS SINS"

"Does Jesus only enable me to 'make the cut' when I die? Or to know what to protest, or how to vote or agitate or organize? It is good to know that when I die all will be well, but is there any good news for life? If I had to choose, I would rather have a car that runs than good insurance on one that doesn't. Can I not have both?"[240]

Just the other day I read a bumper sticker that said: "Working for God on earth doesn't pay much. But His retirement plan is out of this world."

As I read the words I shook my head. I couldn't have disagreed more.

I'm sure such a saying was not ill-intended, but I believe it is misinformed and misleading. In truth, the gospel is about *life*, not death. It is for *living*, not dying. And so if we simply await our "retirement plan" of eternal life then we are overlooking what God longs to do in our lives in the mean time. We are forfeiting the life we were intended.

Jesus clearly said that He is *"not the God of the dead but of the living."*[241] He died not only so that we may be saved from hell, but also so that we may be saved from pride, selfishness, greed, envy, lust, violence, hatred, apathy…and the list goes on. He died for us so that we may live for Him.

"One thing I ask of the Lord,
This is what I seek:
That I may dwell in the house of the Lord
All the days of my life."[242]

After all, eternity is not later. It is not some remote time and place that awaits us on the other side of death. Eternity is *now*.

So, a life wisely lived—a life lived to the full—does not merely sit back and await eternity. Rather, it strives to seize the day. It works to use all of its capabilities and potential. It makes the most of what it has been entrusted.

What We've Been Entrusted

He was a strong man, stern, hardworking and devoted. It was upon these qualities that he began his own business, building it from the ground up. And it was because of these qualities that everyone was surprised when he announced he was leaving on a trip.

He prepared his finest colt for the journey. He packed all that he could carry. Then he called for his three most trusted servants.

The three men shuffled into the room. They each stood nervously in the presence of their master. His departure meant that they would no longer be needed, and so they expected to hear the worst.

But instead of hearing the words they anticipated, their master pointed silently to three wooden chests along the far wall. He walked over to them, leaned down and threw open their lids one by one. The three men's jaws dropped at the sight. They stood awestruck. Speechless. The trunks contained more wealth than their wages could earn in a lifetime.

The servants had expected to be laid off, but instead they were each given a chest of wealth and put in charge of their master's finances while he was absent. They had never before been shown such respect. They had never before been given such an opportunity or responsibility. Amidst their shock, they hardly noticed as their master mounted his colt and galloped away.

Immediately the men took their entrusted wealth and went their separate ways. They each used the money they'd been given in their own particular manner, wondering when their master would return. But as the weeks turned to months and the months turned to years they soon began to wonder whether he'd come back at all.

Then, just as suddenly as he had left their master one day returned. He galloped in and called for the three servants he had entrusted. Once again they shuffled nervously into his presence. They stood together upon the exact spot he'd departed from years before.

The first servant approached him with his head bowed and two shiny trunks in tow. He laid the trunks at his feet and said, "Master, look! You entrusted me with much, and so I have much to offer in return."

His master placed a soft hand on his shoulder and said, "Well done, good and faithful servant!" They embraced one another and he called for a banquet to be thrown in honor of the servant's accomplishments.

The second servant approached him with his head bowed and two more trunks in tow. He also laid the trunks at his feet and said,

BURIED ALIVE: A DISCUSSION ON OVERCOMING THE "SEVEN LIFELESS SINS"

"Master, look! You entrusted me with much, and so I too have much to offer in return."

Again he was met with a soft hand, an embrace, and the words of praise, "Well done, good and faithful servant!" A second celebration was ordered in honor of the servant's success.

But the third servant remained silent. He stood at a distance, scratching in the sand with his toe. Finally, he stepped forward to reveal a single trunk, dull and soiled. He handed it back to his master and said, "Look, you entrusted me with much, but I dug a hole and buried the chest you gave me. So here is what belongs to you."

The master was consumed by disappointment and anger. He shook his head and said, "I entrusted you with this, and you *buried* it? Couldn't you have at least deposited it into a bank and drawn interest? You wicked, lazy servant!"

He then took the chest and handed it to the other two. A grubby chest of forsaken ability and wasted potential. (Matthew 25:14-30)

†

The third man in this familiar parable depicts lifelessness to a tee. He wasn't immoral, he was just lethargic. He wasn't wicked, he was just plain lazy. He didn't use his money for promiscuous or extravagant living. Rather, he did nothing with it at all.

But as Moliere once wrote, "It is not only for what we do that we are held responsible, but also for what we do not do." For that reason, we have no right to forsake all that we have been entrusted. We have no right to waste what we've been given. We have no right to just take this life and bury it.

"Each one should use whatever gift he has received to serve others, faithfully administering God's grace in its various forms."[243]
"Do not neglect your gift."[244]

"Now it is required that those who have been given a trust must prove faithful."[245]

"Offer the parts of your body to Him as instruments of righteousness."[246]

"then if anyone hears the trumpet but does not take warning and the sword comes and takes his life, his blood will be on his own head...But if the watchman sees the sword coming and does not blow the trumpet to warn the people and the sword comes and takes the life of one of them, that man will be taken away because of his sin, but I will hold the watchman accountable for his blood."[247]

"For everyone who has been given much, much will be demanded; and from the one who has been entrusted with much, much more will be asked."[248]

    The apostle James said that anyone *"who knows the good he ought to do and doesn't do it, sins."*[249] And Paul described such men as godless and wicked who worked to *"suppress the truth."*[250] So, just as the servants in this parable knew what their master expected of them, we know the expectation of ours. As a result, "You wicked, lazy servant" seems like a just response for any of us who live lifelessly. It is a just response for any life branded by laziness.
    However, envision the contrary.
    Imagine a life lived in Christ, for Christ. Imagine a life lived where we care more about the earthly wellbeing and eternal future of others than we do our own day to day schedule. Imagine a life that so brilliantly reflects the love and light of Jesus Christ that anyone we meet cannot keep from seeing His beauty.
    Now, imagine on the day of judgment when your master—the God of the universe—looks upon you and speaks the sweetest words you have ever heard, words more satisfying and gratifying than you could ever imagine, words that quench your heart and soul for all of eternity:
    "Well done, good and faithful servant!"

Ridiculous Laziness

    It's impossible to imagine what those words would sound like. Would they be audible at all, or would they be more like a feeling deep in your bones that swells in your heart until you get goose bumps on the back of your neck and then all over your body? I have no idea. But I believe the closest I will ever come to experiencing them in this lifetime recently occurred...

BURIED ALIVE: A DISCUSSION ON OVERCOMING THE "SEVEN LIFELESS SINS"

What I'm talking about is a recent visit to Victoria Falls, one of the world's Seven Natural Wonders. It measures over a mile wide (5,567 feet), and is nearly twice as tall as Niagara. It is breathtakingly huge; truly indescribable.

A small bridge spans the gorge directly in front of the roaring cascade. And so on a cool afternoon in June, I walked out to its center and stood face to face with the largest waterfall in the world.

The sound was deafening. Consuming. I can still hear it to this day.

The view was incredible. From where I stood I couldn't see anything beyond the stretch of the falls. Multiple rainbows curved around me in every direction, arching over the bridge I stood on and circling around to make complete circles. I had never seen anything like it.

The sensation was overwhelming. Cascading waters rained down on me, soaking through my shirt and shoes. Entrepreneurs had tried to sell me a rain coat before I ventured out onto the bridge, but I didn't want to do anything to rob myself of this experience. I wanted to feel it all.

As I stood there my body became numb. My knees weakened and my arms hung limp. I was unable to hear anything over the water's roar. I was unable to see anything beyond the stretch of the falls. I was unable to feel anything except the heart pounding in my chest.

At that moment I felt as though I would never move.

I never wanted to.

†

For many people laziness stems from deficient dreams. Their goals are so lackluster that they fail to inspire, and so they remain fettered by the lifeless sin of laziness simply because they have no ambition to pull them from the mundane. They have no purpose that lifts them above the haze of apathy.

Others seem to never take their souls seriously. They never take the effort to decide what they believe, (as we talked about in the first chapter.) Or else they never decide what they want out of life, (as we discussed in the last chapter.) As a result laziness holds such a firm grip on their life that they actually convince themselves it doesn't matter. They'll worry about it later, they say, as if *life* is no big deal.

Still others have no reason or excuse at all.

They know that they should love more. Yet they don't. They know they should be more into God's word. Yet they're not. They know they need the support and leadership of fellow Christians. Yet when that alarm sounds on Sunday morning it's just too easy to pull the covers up over their head and promise themselves that they'll make it next week.

But honestly, how can you or I claim to love our Lord and then live without love in our lives? How can we believe that the Bible is His word and then go weeks without opening it? How can we expect to live our life to the full if we won't even get out of bed for our Lord?

C. S. Lewis once wrote, "Christianity is a statement which, if true, is of infinite importance, and, if false, is of no importance. The one thing it cannot be is of moderate importance."

You see, none of us are perfect. From seatbelts to caffeine we all have things we know we should do, but don't. Yet to miss out on life simply because we are too lazy to live, that is truly absurd. It is a pitiful barrier between you and me and the life we could have. It is simply ridiculous.

It is like standing before something as breathtaking as Victoria Falls and then covering our eyes to walk away.

More than a Worn Out Cliché

So now what?

In this chapter we've discussed the dangers of laziness, and the need to overcome it in our lives. But what actions can we actually take? It's easy to talk about these things, but what can we *do?*

I imagine we've all heard talk of Christ-like living, and the mantra to love our neighbor as ourselves. Many of us have heard it so many times before that it has grown stale. As a result, the grand idea has become little more than a worn out cliché.

We usually hear the words. Nod in agreement. Then go about our day as if nothing has happened.

But I wonder, how can we move beyond mere nods of agreement? How can you and I truly begin living as Christ instructed? How can we actively avoid lifelessness?

For that reason I leave you with a challenge. I challenge you to list some specific and attainable goals for better loving your spouse and closest friends. List some specific and attainable goals for better loving that annoying colleague at work. List some specific and attainable goals for better loving yourself.

In the last chapter you decided what you want out of this life by writing your own personal mission statement. Now decide how you will actualize that statement. You can use the spaces provided at the end of this chapter, or of course you can write it elsewhere. Like with your mission statement, the most important thing is that you make it your own.

So, pray to God about what He would have you do. Pray about the direction you should take. Pray about how and when and where you should act. Pray. Pray. Pray.

Just don't stop there.

Short Term Goals:

_____
_____
_____
_____
_____

Long Term Goals:

_____
_____
_____
_____
_____
_____

Chapter 7

Tolerance
Fundamentalism
Compromise
Materialism
Busyness
Laziness
Comfort

Comfort

"Beyond all question, the mystery of godliness is great."[251]
—the Apostle Paul

"Holding on and holding it in
Yeah you're working
Building a mystery
And choosing so carefully."
—Sarah McLachlan, "Building a Mystery"

"We cover our deep ignorance with words, but we are ashamed to wonder, we are afraid to whisper 'mystery'."
—A. W. Tozer

I once read a book with some sort of warning stamped across the back cover that read: "Caution! Prepare to meet God."

It wasn't a very good book.

I tell you this because I feel it necessary to offer a warning, yet I don't want it to sound cliché like that book did. I don't like the idea sounding cliché and that's not at all what I'm trying to be. Instead I'm trying to be real.

You see, the pages to come raise some tough questions. They raise questions about Christianity and the Bible. They even raise questions about God. Yet they offer very few answers. They contain no real explanations. And they provide no ultimate solutions.

So as you can see, this chapter may be dangerous for some. It may cause doubt, confusion and frustration. I believe it may actually do your faith more harm than good if you're not ready to dig deeper and to seek truth for yourself.

For that reason, if you had rather stay in the snug safety of your comfort zone then you may not want to read the rest of this chapter.

If you had rather not be challenged or stretched then you may want to stop now. I'll just meet you again on page 186, and we can pretend this whole thing never happened.

As for the rest of us…You've been warned…

The Most Important Chapter of This Entire Book

I believe that God longs to comfort His children. Scripture calls Christ *"the Father of compassion and the God of all comfort."*[252] And in the book of Matthew Jesus says, *"Come to me, all you who are weary and burdened, and I will give you rest…For my yoke is easy and my burden is light."*[253]

But like a woman who loves her rose over her rose bearer, it seems we often value our comfort over our comforter. We place the "I will give you rest" before the "come to me." And so rather than seeking comfort *in* Christ, we seek comfort *instead* of Christ.

In fact, the Barna Research group recently surveyed Americans by asking them to rank 21 different life goals in order of importance. It discovered that "desiring to have a close, personal relationship with God ranks just sixth among the 21 life goals tested, trailing such desires as 'living a comfortable lifestyle.'"[254]

Teenagers that were surveyed ranked comfort above such goals as a 'clear purpose for living', 'high integrity', and even having a 'close relationship with God'.[255] — It seems we had rather be confused on our purpose for living, have low integrity and be distant from God, as long as we are comfortable!

Many Americans call themselves Christians, yet according to statistics like these it seems that few want God to actually affect their lives. In truth, they don't want to be stretched. They don't want to be challenged. And for heavens sake, they don't want to be made uncomfortable. C. S. Lewis articulates this mindset of so many Christians today by writing:

> "An 'impersonal God' — well and good. A subjective God of beauty, truth and goodness, inside our own heads — even better…But God Himself, alive, pulling at the other end of the cord, perhaps approaching at an infinite speed, the hunter, king, husband — that is quite another matter…There comes a moment when people who have been dabbling in religion…suddenly draw back. Supposing we really found

BURIED ALIVE: A DISCUSSION ON OVERCOMING THE "SEVEN LIFELESS SINS"

Him? We never meant it to come to *that!*"[256]

You see, the desire for comfort is what often keeps us from a deeper commitment to God. It keeps us from change. It keeps us from questioning ourselves and our perspectives, from taking risk and moving beyond ourselves. Ultimately, it keeps us from *life*.

For that reason I believe this discussion may be the most important chapter of this entire book. For if we refuse to move beyond ourselves then nothing in our discussion of tolerance or fundamentalism will make a difference. If we refuse to think outside our spiritual and theological comfort zones then nothing in our discussion of compromise or materialism is relevant. And if we refuse to challenge the way we live and think then nothing in our discussion of busyness or laziness matters. In the words of King Solomon, "*All of them are meaningless, a chasing after the wind.*"[257]

†

So, having said all of that, I can't think of a better place to begin than by making us all a little uncomfortable...

Scripture You Won't Likely Hear Preached on this Sunday at Church

"Because of their sinful deeds, I will drive them out of my house. I will no longer love them."[258]

"Just as it is written: 'Jacob I loved, but Esau I hated.'"[259]

"I tell you the truth, all the sins and blasphemies of men will be forgiven them. But whoever blasphemies against the Holy Spirit will never be forgiven; he is guilty of an eternal sin."[260]

"blasphemy against the Spirit will not be forgiven."[261]

"A man ought not to cover his head, since he is the image and glory of God; but the woman is the glory of man...she should cover her head."[262]

"Now if there is no resurrection, what will those do who are baptized for the dead? If the dead are not raised at all, why are people baptized for them?"[263]

"Do not spare them; put to death men and women, children and infants."[264]

"...kill, without showing pity or compassion. Slaughter old men, young men and maidens, women and children."[265]

"He whose testicles are crushed or whose male member is cut off shall not enter the assembly of the Lord. No bastards shall enter the assembly of the Lord; even to the tenth generation none of his descendants shall enter the assembly of the Lord."[266]

"But Onan knew that the offspring would not be his; so whenever he lay with his brother's wife, he spilled his semen on the ground to keep from producing offspring for his brother. What he did was wicked in the Lord's sight; so He put him to death also."[267]

"If in spite of this you still do not listen to me but continue to be hostile toward me...You will eat the flesh of your sons and the flesh of your daughters."[268]

†

It may surprise you to read a list like that in a book like this. As a Christian you're probably used to hearing scripture about God's unconditional love, not scripture on how He hated Esau. You're probably used to hearing sermons on His unlimited grace, not scripture on unforgivable sin. And you're probably used to reading books on Christ's compassion, not scripture on how God called for the genocide of an entire people.

But why?

Why is it so surprising and rare to read challenging and difficult scripture? Why is it that we avoid the parts of the Bible that makes us uncomfortable? Why do we patronize our own faith by surrounding ourselves with scripture to reinforce it? These are the kinds of verses that skeptics are familiar with, so why do we as Christians often deny their existence?

Honestly, I don't understand what Jesus meant when He said blasphemy against the Holy Spirit was unforgivable. I'm not sure why Paul's words often seem so chauvinistic. And I have no idea what it means to be "baptized for the dead."

But the point is that you and I can not say we believe the Bible and then gloss over the parts we don't prefer. We can't argue for its literal truth and then ignore those verses that we don't like, or that contradict our personal theologies.

Well, we can, I guess. In fact that is exactly what I did for the first half of my life. I would read a list like this or hear similar claims from an unbeliever and I would become overwhelmed. After all, I'm not a theologian. I didn't attend seminary. And so I would dismiss any questions that arose. I would promise to think about them later. Or I would convince myself they weren't really that important, all the while turning my back to a deeper walk with Christ.

It was all very pathetic. Very lifeless.

When I wasn't dismissing or ignoring scripture I was usually combating it. It took a lot of dedication and practice, but over the years I became rather skilled at wrestling scripture into submission. I would read a verse that confused me and I'd instinctively start making excuses and justifications, trying to explain away what it truly said. I would twist and skew and push and cram until I finally fit Paul's words into my own preconceived theology.

It was very dumb of me. Lifeless indeed.

I believe that dismissing scripture and combating scripture are the two most common responses to difficult Bible passages. I've done it myself more times than I'm likely to admit, and I've seen others do it time and again, often without even realizing it.

But recently I've come see that there is a third option. With it there is no need to close our eyes and run from the truth. There is no need for excuses or justifications, and there is no twisting or skewing or cramming involved. Instead, there is only personal humility and intellectual honesty.

God & Logic

I say intellectual honesty because I believe that is what Christianity today needs more than anything. I think it has been the enemy's greatest tool to convince contemporary Christians their faith must be blind. As a result, many of us today seem to see God and logic as conflicting forces.

We hear scientific debates, a skeptic's inquiry, or scripture like in the list above and instead of searching for answers we flee from them.

Our mind shuts down. Our heels dig in. And then we say something like, "You've just got to have faith."

But since when did having faith mean you couldn't think for yourself?

Since when did being spiritual mean being stupid?

After the Super Bowl my friends and I were watching *The Simpsons* when something happened that illustrates this point perfectly. The Simpson family has a Christian neighbor named Ned Flanders, and in this particular episode Ned decided to make a home movie about the Old Testament. He dressed his two sons in robes and sandals, set his camera up in the back yard, and started to film. But just as the scene began one of his sons turned to Ned and asked, "Dad, if God made Adam and Eve where did the rest of the people come from? Did Adam and Eve have sex with their children, or did their children have sex with each other?"

It was an honest question.—A question we have probably all had at one point or another. But sadly, most of us were probably met with an answer like the one Ned Flanders delivered. After a moment of quiet confusion he said: "Shut up, son, and quit asking stupid questions!"

Everyone else in the room chuckled. I blushed red with embarrassment. I felt embarrassed and even ashamed because the scene struck a chord within me.

Scripture says to love the Lord with all our heart, soul, strength *and* mind.[269] Yet it seems to me that many Christians—like Ned Flanders—have somehow and for some reason come to view science and logic and intellectual honesty as enemies to their faith. As a result, they've allowed the enemy to monopolize the claim of intellectual thought, leaving Christianity somewhere in the past, in a time before science and reason and rationale.

†

Chase's cousin recently moved in with his girlfriend. They're not married but they're trying to save money on rent. It's caused quite a drama within his family, with opinions and tempers flaring. The fire still is far from dying.

Anyway, a few of us were driving around the city the other day when I began to think out loud, saying, "You know, even if it weren't for religious reasons I don't think I'd want to move in with a girlfriend. I mean, even if we ended up together just think how that would spoil the anticipation and excitement and madness of marriage. Instead of saying 'I do' and then coming home to my wife and a whole new kind of reality, I would say 'I do' and then just come home to her *again.* There'd be a lot of the magic lost, I think. — A lot of the thrill."

The rest nodded in agreement. I remember thinking I had made a pretty good point.

But then just yesterday we were all together again, sitting outside on Chase's deck, when he picked up the conversation where we'd left it four days prior. He took a deep breath and exhaled slowly and then began by commenting on how we as Christians too often separate God and logic as if they were two opposing things. "We say things like 'even if it weren't for religious reasons', and then we lay out a logical rationale. It seems we often fail to realize that the logical reason *is* the religious reason."

He paused to draw another breath, reflecting on his own words. We all leaned in closer. He continued, "I don't think God just made up a bunch of rules for the fun of it. I think He knows that drugs can ravage our minds and He knows premarital sex will dull our hearts. He understands the way we're wired, and so He knows better than we do what is truly best for us. — What will give us the greatest thrill."

The rest of us nodded in agreement. I remember thinking he had made an ever better point.

†

You see, God gave us minds for a reason. — So that we could learn and grow in Him, and better ourselves and help others. But if you and I separate our minds from our faith then how can we ever really do any of this?

In truth, it is only when we begin using our minds that we may fully and truly begin using our hearts. Then when we're faced with challenges we won't have to say, "You've just got to have faith" and then turn to run away. Instead, we'll be able to say, "You know, I can't pretend to have all the answers, but *this* what my faith means to me…*This* is what I believe…And *this* is why…"

The Third Option: Embracing Scripture, Embracing God

By saying all of this I'm not implying that by using our heads we'll be able to figure out our God. Not at all. In fact, I'm implying quite the opposite.

The truth is that the more honest we are with ourselves about God, His word, and our faith, the more we'll realize how little we know. We'll recognize that there is a lot to Christianity and to life that confuses us. We'll come to see that God is greater than the god we've made Him out to be. In the end, the only option left open to us will be to embrace a God too great for our minds to comprehend.

†

The Bible is a beautiful thing. If you take my advice from chapter 5 and find a comfy chair to meditate with it I'm sure you'll come to the same conclusion. There is something pure and true and refreshing about the scriptures. The more you read them the more they will move and stir and breathe throughout your life.

That is why our sinful nature so often flees from the Bible. That is why we find it so difficult to open it at times, yet we'll read an insignificant paper back novel at the drop of a whim. It makes me think that the last thing the enemy wants you or I to do is read God's word.

But having said that, I believe the last thing God wants us to do is read His word without being intellectually honest.

You see, the enemy tries to keep us from God's word, but if he cannot do that then he seeks at least to keep us from what God's word truly says. He fills our minds with predetermined ideas so that we see what we want to see rather than the picture that's truly before us. As a result we often hear our own voice rather than the true voice of God whispering at our soul.

For this reason we must learn to accept scripture for what it is rather than what we want it to be. And instead of dismissing it or wrestling it into subjection we must learn to embrace it. Read the following verse and see for yourself what I mean. Its context is found in the second chapter of 1 Timothy:

BURIED ALIVE: A DISCUSSION ON OVERCOMING THE "SEVEN LIFELESS SINS"

"And Adam was not the one deceived; it was the woman who was deceived and became a sinner. But women will be saved through childbearing—if they continue in faith, love and holiness with propriety."[270]

As you read this verse did you instinctively dismiss it? Did you begin to combat it? Or were you able to accept the fact that you're uncertain what Paul truly and completely meant?

That is what it means to embrace scripture with intellectual honesty. It's not that we must throw up our hands and stop seeking the truth of scripture. Edmund Burke once said, "Nobody makes a greater mistake than he who does nothing because he could only do a little." In the same way, to forsake theology because we'll never have the perfect one, or to abandon God because we'll never see His full face in this lifetime would be the greatest mistake of our lives.

No, the point is not that we should give up.

The point is that we must finally give *in*.

We must stop fighting the unknown, pretending to have all the answers. We must accept the Bible for what it says rather than for what we want it to say. In the end, we must look past our theological confinements and move toward that vast abyss of wonder and awe and admiration that awaits us just beyond. For it is only there, in the great beyond, that He can be truly found.[271]

Your Spouse is Not an Encyclopedia (& Neither is God)

I used to argue for the literal truth of Scripture.

In between dismissing and combating the verses that I didn't like I would argue with anyone who'd listen why and how the Bible was literal. But since learning to embrace Scripture I've realized that arguing for its literal truth does Scripture a great injustice.

The Bible is true. It is alive. It is real. It is powerful. It is vital. It is authoritative. It is timeless. It is priceless. It is eternal. It is mysterious. It is divine. It is inspired. It is the voice of God. It is beyond my understanding in more ways than I can understand. It moves. It breathes. It is beautiful.

But it is not literal.

I think most people who say this have their heart in the right place.

I think I did. But I don't think they know what they are truly saying. I know I didn't.

In fact, I doubt anyone actually believes the Bible is literal. Even if they hold to a literal creation story of seven days and a literal decree for women to remain quiet, they surely don't extend this literal lens to all of scripture. If they did then that would mean God is a lamb[272], Satan is a lion[273], and in order for you or I to follow Christ we'd first have to be consumed by fire.[274] From Genesis to Revelations the Bible is filled with word imagery and metaphors. For that reason it seems that the word literal is about the absolute *worst* word we as Christians could use to describe it.

So, arguing with an unbeliever over Scripture's literality can actually do their faith more harm than good. That's because by definition they are right! If you're intent on arguing then, please, pick a different adjective.

A literal view of scripture can harm your faith as well. That's because we as Christians often start seeing the Bible as some sort of holy reference book rather than an ancient collection of poems, songs, stories and prophecies. We begin to approach it for answers and quick fixes rather than for spiritual truth and revelation.

And so, when we encounter questions rather than solutions and find heartfelt humanity rather than cold statistics we often don't know what to do with them. We usually end up ignoring these verses all together, or we pound them into submission like I once did. Then we move on in search of the answers we came looking for; the answers that we want to hear; the answers that fit into our preexistent understanding.

But God's word is not a how-to list, and it is not a book of easy answers. In truth, it is more like a song than it is a dictionary. It is a spiritual book, and so it must be read in a spiritual manner.

Consider this next list and see for yourself:

• In the book of Genesis chapter 1 God makes the beasts of the earth first and then man, but in Genesis chapter 2 He makes man first and then the beasts.[275]

• In the book of 1 Kings Solomon has forty thousand stalls of horses, but in 2 Chronicles Solomon has only four thousand stalls.[276]

BURIED ALIVE: A DISCUSSION ON OVERCOMING THE "SEVEN LIFELESS SINS"

- In the book of 2 Samuel God tells David there will be seven years of famine, but in I Chronicles He tells David there will be three years.[277]

- In the book of 1 Samuel Saul kills himself, but 2 Samuel one of David's men kills Saul.[278]

- In the book of Luke Satan tempts Jesus by first taking Him to a high mountain and then to the temple pinnacle, but in Matthew Satan takes Jesus first to the temple pinnacle and then to a high mountain.[279]

- In the book of Mark Jesus clearly instructs his disciples to take a staff, but in the books of Luke and Matthew He clearly says not to.[280]

- In the book of Matthew Jesus cleanses the temple on the first day, but in the book of Mark He looks around the temple, leaves, and then comes back the following day to cleanse it.[281]

- In the books of Matthew and Mark it takes only six days for Jesus to lead Peter, James and John up the mountain, but in Luke it takes eight days.[282]

- In the book of Matthew Jesus is given wine mingled with gall while He is hanging on the cross, but in Mark He is given wine mingled with myrrh.[283]

- In the book of Matthew Mary Magdalene and the other Mary go to the tomb of Christ, but in the book of Mark it is Mary Magdalene, Mary the mother of James, and Salome who go, and in the book of John it is only Mary Magdalene.[284]

- In the book of Matthew an angel of the Lord is sitting on the stone outside Christ's empty tomb, but in the book of Mark there is a young man inside the tomb, in the book of Luke there are two men, and in the book John there are two angels.[285]

- In the books of Matthew, Luke and John those who witness Christ's empty tomb run and report it to the disciples, but in the book of Mark they remain quiet out of fear.[286]

- In the book of Matthew it clearly says that Judas died by hanging himself, but in the book of Acts it seems that Judas died by falling headlong.[287]

As it turns out, there seem to be several contradictions within the Bible. Just like any time you have different people telling the same story there are dozens of minor, trivial discrepancies.

The point is, *what difference does it truly make?*

Again, that is what it means to embrace Scripture. For if we want to move beyond a lifeless sort of spirituality then you and I can no longer ignore or deny the presence of these contradictions. And we must no longer explain them away. Instead, I believe it is time that the Christian community finally accepted this reality. Then maybe we could move on to consider what there is to be learned from it.

After all, God certainly could have created a book devoid of contradiction if He wished. *But maybe there is something to be learned from the fact that He didn't.* Maybe there is some relevance to this idea of the Bible being a spiritual and relational thing after all!

Besides, what does it matter that in the book of Mark Jesus says to take a staff and then in the books of Luke and Matthew he says not to? What difference does it really make if Judas hung himself, fell headlong, both, or neither?

It seems that Christianity today is so scared for Scripture to breathe, and so afraid that God will move beyond its puny understandings, that many of us have been fighting an unnecessary battle. We've become so busy dismissing and combating Scripture that we've missed its true point entirely. We've become so wrapped up in the words that we've overlooked their meaning. We've become so hung up in the irrelevant details that we've ignored the truth and the beauty they have to offer.

†

BURIED ALIVE: A DISCUSSION ON OVERCOMING THE "SEVEN LIFELESS SINS"

I heard a story recently that articulates this point beautifully. The story was about a student, a holy man, and his dog.

One day the student joined the holy man as he and his dog took their nightly stroll. After a few short minutes the student began to ask about difficulties and contradictions he had found while reading Scripture. The holy man nodded as the student spoke, as if he understood precisely. It was almost as if he too had once struggled with the same questions.

After taking a few more steps, preparing his words with care, the holy man began to speak. "You must understand," he said, "That words are only guideposts. Never let them get in the way of truth."

With that the man stopped and looked down at his dog. "Fetch me the moon," he said, pointing to the full moon overhead. He then turned back to the student and asked, "Where is my dog looking?"

"He's looking at your finger."

"Exactly. Don't confuse the guideposts with the truth they are pointing to. Don't be like my dog."

†

Honestly, treating Scripture like an encyclopedia works about as well as treating your spouse like one. You might be able to find out their birth date and even their favorite color. If you're lucky you might find a picture. But could you possibly conceive the way they make you feel when you are in their presence? Could you laugh yourself to tears over an inside joke you share? Could you really know them at all?

That is the way it is with God. The Bible is not an encyclopedia or an almanac or a dictionary. And so, if you and I persist to treat it that way then a distant, lifeless, dictionary sort of understanding is all we will ever know of our Maker.

We may read that He is love. But we will never experience what His love feels like.

We may read that He strong. But we will never understand what it means to have His strength pulsing through our lives.

And we may read that He sent His only Son. But we will never know the truth and mystery and wonder of what that really means.

"You diligently study the Scriptures because you think that by them you possess eternal life. These are Scriptures that testify about Me, yet you refuse to come to Me to have life."[288]

The Worship of Wonder

The effects of all of this—dismissing Scripture, combating Scripture, treating Scripture like an encyclopedia—has had a very severe effect on Christianity today. If you just look at the average church marquee you'll see what I mean. Yesterday I drove around the city, investigating for myself what these signs had to say. Here are a few samples I found:

- "Prevent truth decay. Brush up on the Bible"
- "Stop, Drop & Roll won't work in Hell"
- "God answers knee mail"
- "Wal-Mart isn't the only saving place"
- "Forbidden fruit creates many jams"
- "The best vitamin for a Christian is B1"

Of course, there's nothing wrong with being clever or cute. But as I drove home I began to wonder whether is was really necessary to relegate our Lord to this level. We all need a little humor and we all could use a good laugh. But have you ever considered how such clichés must appear to unbelievers? (Let me give you a hint: They're not laughing *with* us.) Seriously, the marquee outside your local McDonalds is probably more sophisticated than any of these examples.

A. W. Tozer once wrote, "Low views of God destroy the gospel for all who hold them…The essence of idolatry is the entertainment of thoughts about God that are unworthy of Him." Tozer goes on to conclude, "The heaviest obligation lying upon the Christian Church today is to purify and elevate her concept of God until it is once more worthy of Him—and of her."[289]

Nevertheless, it seems that we've become so comfortable in our spiritual walks, so frightened of being frightened and so uncertain of uncertainty, that we've created some sort of toddler religion devoid of all complexity and complication, wonder and worth.

BURIED ALIVE: A DISCUSSION ON OVERCOMING THE "SEVEN LIFELESS SINS"

†

I was reminded of this truth again when I recently met Danny for breakfast. Over a steaming cup of coffee and a hot plate of pancakes he asked me what I would think if the second coming of Jesus Christ suddenly occurred. His question caught me off guard. And so in a moment of complete, transparent honesty I looked him in the eye and said:

"It would scare the crap out of me!"

My answer seemed to surprise him.—Not to mention it spawned a healthy conversation about God. I think it surprised him and actually made him want to discuss my Christian beliefs because it was not the pat answer he was used to hearing from evangelical Christians.

You see, most Christians I know think they must answer certain questions in certain ways, more like regurgitating arithmetic tables than being transparent, because they are more concerned with the right answer than the real answer. As a result, they can never have doubts. They can never think or question outside of the box. They can never admit confusion, disappointment or fear. In essence, they can never be *honest*.

But I think anyone—believers and unbelievers alike—who say they never have doubts about their beliefs is either dead or dumb. Anyone who never thinks outside of the box will forever be imprisoned by it. And anyone who says they wouldn't be scared senseless if they suddenly found themselves face to face with God is worshiping a pretty small god.

"When I was a child, I talked like a child, I thought like a child, I reasoned like a child. When I became a man, I put childish ways behind me." [290]

"In fact, though by this time you ought to be teachers, you need someone to teach you the elementary truths of God's word all over again. You need milk, not solid food!" [291]

"leave the elementary teachings about Christ and go on to maturity." [292]

"Then we will no longer be infants, tossed back and forth by the waves, and blown here and there by every wind of teaching and by the cunning and craftiness of men in their deceitful scheming."[293]

"stop thinking like children."[294]

Donald Miller, one of my favorite authors, seems to understand the dangers of pat answers and Christian clichés. He writes in his book *Blue Like Jazz*, one of my favorite books, "The more I climb outside my pat answers, the more invigorating the view, the more my heart enters into worship." He continues by saying that "Too much of our time is spent trying to chart God on a grid and too little is spent allowing our hearts to feel awe. By reducing Christian spirituality to formula, we deprive our hearts of wonder...I don't think there's any better worship than wonder."[295]

What a beautiful observation. I couldn't agree more. Despite the solace of our theological comfort zones, I believe we must allow more room for the worship of wonder.

Only then will God become more to us than a formula. He will become more than a point to be proven or a case to be argued. He will become more than a hollowed idea or a trivialized theology, explainable in eight words or less on our local church marquee.

Instead, He will come to life in your life. He will become real and fresh and true. In the end, He will become truly—finally—'Godly.'

A God Too Great

In truth, there is a lot in the bible that confuses me, and there is a lot about God I don't know. I can admit that now. Years ago I couldn't. To do so I thought was a sign of ignorance or a lack of faith. So instead of seeking truth for myself I simply accepted the answers religion handed me, and instead of seeking with my whole heart I learned to silence it.

But I believe we've held God at a distance for long enough. I believe it is time we let Him out of our theological confinements. It is time we felt Him and touched Him and experienced Him for ourselves.

So, if you are a pastor I plea and pray that you will no longer shelter your congregation. And if you are a member of the congregation I plea and pray that you will no longer shelter your soul.

BURIED ALIVE: A DISCUSSION ON OVERCOMING THE "SEVEN LIFELESS SINS"

After all, I had rather accept the fact that God is too great for my mind to understand than to create my own god small enough to comprehend.

†

For this reason I leave you with yet another list. In chapter 2 a similar list was offered to make the point we haven't all of life's answers. Now I offer it as a challenge; as another way to escape the lifelessness of your comfort zone.

Look over it, ponder it, and meditate on it. Then begin to explore possible responses. It could be a great opportunity to meet with friends for a discussion, or perhaps you had rather explore possibilities with your pastor or mentor. Each question is broad and rich enough to lend hours of conversation.

The only rule is that you don't look for answers. Don't look to support your own theology. Don't look for a debate. Instead, look for possibilities. Look for insight and understanding. Look for *God*.

If you do you may be amazed by what you discover. You may be stretched. You may be challenged. You may even experience a frightening new depth of spirituality.

…Just don't say I didn't warn you.

1. What is the proper role for women in church? Do you believe they should be allowed to teach men or other women? Have you ever had an experience with a woman pastor or teacher? Or if you are woman, have you ever taught in church?[296]

2. What should be done about homosexuality and the way we're handling it? What changes should be made? Do you believe homosexuals should be allowed to marry or to be ordained? Why or why not?

Did you know that after his death the classic and beloved Christian author Henry Nouwin was discovered to have struggled with homosexual tendencies for his entire life? How does this fact change your perception of homosexuality?[297]

3. Do you believe someone can ever lose their salvation? If so, then how? What if someone renounces their faith in God and Christ?[298]

4. What do you believe about evolution and the age of the universe? How do you interpret the creation stories of Genesis? Do you believe science and scripture are contradictory, or can they be reconciled with one another? Are you familiar with 2 Peter 3:8? What is your answer to the "stupid question" Ned's son asked?[299]

5. What are your beliefs on marriage in light of what scripture teaches about adultery? Why has divorce become such an accepted occurrence within the church today while other marital taboos remain harshly unaccepted?[300]

6. What do you believe happens to an infant who dies without ever having the opportunity to hear or comprehend the saving grace of Jesus Christ? What about salvation for those with severe mental retardation? And why do our theologies so often excuse these souls from eternal damnation, yet we refuse to do so for others?
(Such as persons living in remote and extreme locations)[301]

7. What do you believe about speaking in tongues? Is it pertinent to salvation, as some denominations believe? Have you ever experienced it personally?[302]

8. How important are other religious traditions such as baptism, communion and circumcision? Are they essential to salvation? What role do they play in the contemporary church? What other traditions do you feel are essential, and what traditions do you feel have been overstated?[303]

9. What do you believe about predestination? Do you and I have free will or did God predetermine who would and who wouldn't worship Him? If God is sovereign where does the extent of His control over our lives end?[304]

10. What are your beliefs on spiritual warfare? Are there instances of demonic possession today, as there were in Jesus' time? Is there an entirely other world of spiritual battle that is unseen to us? If so, then how does all of this reconcile with God's absolute power?[305]

11. What do you think about animal rights? What does scripture mean when it says that we have 'dominion' over the earth? What responsibilities does that come with?[306]

12. What responsibilities do we have to care for our environment? Is our gluttonous way of life disrespectful and even sinful? If so, what practical actions can you and I take? Why are political issues such as abortion and gay rights considered to be so important to Christianity, yet environmental concerns continue to be ignored?[307]

13. What do you believe should be done to care for impoverished nations? As a nation what steps should we take? As a church what steps should we take? As an individual what steps should you take?[308]

14. What do you think about rewards in heaven?[309]

15. What should be done about gun control and capital punishment? Is it right to execute someone for having killed someone else? What legislative changes do you believe should be made?[310]

16. What power do you believe prayer has? Can our words affect a sovereign God? In what ways have you experienced the power of prayer first hand?[311]

17. What are your beliefs on birth control and medically assisted pregnancy? Are these advancements acceptable to use, or do they challenge God's design and intent?[312]

18. What are your beliefs on stem cell research? Have you researched the issue? If so, then do you think it should be allowed? Why or why not?[313]

19. How do you believe the Bible should be properly interpreted?[314]

20. What does Scripture mean when it refers to Israel as God's chosen people? What does that mean for the nation of Israel today? Is it still God's chosen people, or have we all been made part of God's family through the sanctification of Jesus Christ? In the end will all Jews be reunited with God?[315]

21. What do you believe about the end times? Do you believe we will experience them in our lifetime? Will the rapture of Christians occur before or after the time of tribulation? How much have your beliefs about the end times been shaped by the popular Left Behind series of fictional books?[316]

22. Why do bad things happen to good people? Why does a God of love allow so much pain and suffering in this world?[317]

23. What do you believe happens to people in remote locations and cultures who die without ever hearing the good news of Jesus Christ? Are they judged accordingly, or are they unequivocally banished to eternal damnation?[318]

Epilogue

"Ask and it will be given to you; seek and you will find; knock and the door will be opened to you."[319]

—Jesus of Nazareth

"Oh yeah, life goes on
Long after the thrill of livin' is gone
Oh yeah, life goes on
Long after the thrill of livin' is gone they walk on."

—John Mellencamp

"I always remember an epitaph which is in the cemetery at Tombstone, Arizona. It says: 'Here lies Jack Williams. He done his damnedest.' I think that is the greatest epitaph a man can have."

—Harry S. Truman

    Have you ever noticed that no matter how nice of a home you make for it, the turtle will still spend all of its time trying to get out of the box?

    I found Shelby—as he so lovingly became known—along a creek behind my childhood home. I was only nine at the time, and so I "rescued" him from all the perils of the forest. I lavished him with the biggest cardboard box my bike could carry and I built for him an oasis of grass and dirt; an Eden of rocks and sticks.

    But no matter how hard I tried, Shelby was not impressed.

    He turned his shell to the lake front property I'd given him and worked relentlessly to climb those cardboard walls. He met my generous hand each time by rudely retreating his head into his own shell. And when I'd lift him up from the glorious new home I'd made for him his little legs would start moving so feverishly you'd think he might swim right through the air to freedom.

You see, Shelby longed for the creak's fresh, running waters. He longed for the simple fellowship of his turtle friends. And when the monotony of that cardboard existence became too great he even longed for the danger his forest home promised.

Shelby knew that he was meant for more. He would not be fooled. He would not settle. He would not be satisfied.

…If only you and I would be so ambitious.

The Choice Is Yours or Our Cardboard Worlds

Thirty years. That was how long he had lived in his paralytic state; unable to walk, unable to dress or bathe himself, unable to make a living wage of his own. Thirty years. His entire life.

Then one day God showed up. Literally.

The paraplegic was leaning against a marble colonnade that surrounded the pools of Bethesda. He had spent the majority of his days this way—begging and pleading, trading his dignity for cheap change—when suddenly he was approached by an uncommon Stranger.

Strangers usually shuffled by him. They were eager to move on and were sure to never make eye contact. But this One was different. This One paused, looked the man deep in his eyes, and then asked him a question.

"Do you want to get well?"

The man was left speechless. No one had asked him such an obvious question before. In fact, he'd been in this condition for so long that he couldn't remember the last time he'd asked the question himself.

"Do you want to get well?"

The query echoed through the man's mind as he began to describe his situation to the Stranger. But Jesus seemed not to hear his excuses and explanations. Instead He knelt at the man's side and drew Himself closer. Jesus' eyes were serious, almost stern, as the question continued to resonate through them. His lips could hardly restrain a smile.

"Do you want to get well?" (John 5:1-15)

BURIED ALIVE: A DISCUSSION ON OVERCOMING THE "SEVEN LIFELESS SINS"

†

I find it fascinating that Jesus Christ, the all knowing God of our universe, would look a desperate man in the face and ask the most obvious question in the world. But as I think of my own life and the desperate state I often find myself in, I can almost hear Him asking me the same.

You see, we have shared quite a discussion during the past few hundred pages. We've discussed what it means to be lifeless. We've even discussed possible ways to overcome it. But now, as I look back over my own words, I realize that none of it really matters unless you and I *want* to get well.

The journey of a lifetime is now lying before us. The safari of life is now within our grasp. But unless you and I choose—unless we *dare*—to move beyond the confines of our cardboard worlds we will forever be imprisoned by them. Unless we choose life over lifelessness we will forever be buried alive.

In truth it seems that the greatest tragedy in many of our lives is the life we refuse to live. For that reason you and I are now faced with a simple alternative…

We can either choose to stand strong for our beliefs, or we can choose *tolerance*. We can either choose to live and love and to dance with the Divine, or we can choose *fundamentalism*. We can either choose to take responsibility for our sinful selves, or we can choose to *compromise*. We can either choose to let loose of this finite world and to take hold of eternity, or we can choose *materialism*. We can either choose to enjoy this ridiculous thing we call life, or we can choose *busyness*. We can either choose to live each and every day to the full, or we can choose *laziness*. And lastly, we can either choose to stretch our spiritual selves with honesty and admiration and wonder and awe, or we can choose *comfort*.

In the end the choice is yours.

In truth, it always has been.

Questions for Further Discussion

Introduction

1. I doubt that any of us are eager to admit we're buried alive. However, if you were to be completely candid, how "alive" would you say that you are?

2. Does the following metaphor speak to your present life in any way? Why or why not?

> "…As a result, many of our lives are like the fairgrounds a day after the carnival has left town. You can almost hear the laughter of children playing. You can almost see the rides and games and crowds of people. You can almost smell the hotdogs, and taste the funnel cakes.
> But not quite.
> Instead you hear only silence. You see an empty field with used napkins and torn ticket stubs blowing past like tumbleweed. You smell the remnants of a day gone by, and you taste the eerie absence of something missing." (page 8)

3. What kind of expectations did you have in your youth that have yet to transpire? Be specific.

4. What sort of surprises or disappointments has life handed you through the years? Be honest.

5. In contrast to your everyday routine, have you ever had an experience like my encounter with the elephant, where for a moment you felt truly and fully alive?
Describe that experience. Even more importantly, describe those feelings.

6. In what ways do you believe the "Seven *Lifeless* Sins" are more dangerous than the "Seven Deadly Sins"?

7. Which of the lifeless sins do you feel you suffer most from? In what specific way does this sin rob you of the life you're intended to live?

Chapter 1: Tolerance

1. On the day of your funeral, what words do you believe others will use in describing your life?

2. If it were up to you, list at least 5 adjectives you would *want* others to use in describing your life:

3. Is it hard for you to believe that God still performs miracles today? Why or why not? In what ways have you experienced God in your life?

4. What is the difference between relative and objective truth? Offer an example of each:

5. Explain the following excerpt in your own words:

> "Truth by definition is exclusive. But it seems that our itching ears have embraced their own reality. In the process truth has all but died and has been replaced by our own personal opinions.
> For that reason the word "true" now means nothing more than "true for me." And the words "right" and "wrong" are meaningless." (page 24)

6. Have you ever noticed Jesus being used as an opportunity to right off unbelievers rather than an opportunity to embrace them? When? How?

7. When and how have you found yourself more concerned with pleasing others than living your life with truth and integrity? Give specific examples.

Chapter 2: Fundamentalism

1. Would the type of Christianity you see around you be best described as "unbridled and free…synonymous with pleasure and wonder and hope"? (page 40) If not, then what adjectives would you use to describe it?

BURIED ALIVE: A DISCUSSION ON OVERCOMING THE "SEVEN LIFELESS SINS"

2. As Christians how should we handle the issue of alcohol? Do you believe that drinking is right or wrong? Why or why not, and in what way? Where is the line of drunken debauchery drawn?
What about smoking?

What about cursing and the use of obscenities?

What about tattoos?

What about R rated films?

What about secular music?

3. Do you have any friends or family members that are homosexual?
How should the church, as Christ's bride, handle the issue of homosexuality?
How should we, as followers of Christ, handle the issue of homosexuality?

4. What does it mean to "love as an end"? (page 47) What are some sensible and practical ways you can begin doing so?

5. What did C. S. Lewis mean when he penned this poem?

"He whom I bow only know to whom I bow
When I attempt the ineffable Name, murmuring Thou…

Thus always, taken at their word, all prayers blaspheme
Worshipping with frail images a folk-lore dream…

And all men are idolaters, crying unheard
To a deaf idol, if Thou take them at their word." (page 49)

6. What does it mean to "accept the reality of relativity *within* the absolute framework of Christianity"? (page 51)

7. Sir Winston Churchill once said, "Men occasionally stumble over the truth, but most of them pick themselves up and hurry on as if nothing had happened." (page 61)

So, what in this chapter has caused you to stumble? What has challenged or stretched you?

Chapter 3: Compromise

1. Do you think that the general morals of society are in decline? Why?

2. If so, what can we as Christians do about it?

3. If you were to be completely honest, how would you answer the following series of questions?

> "...imagine this: A party is thrown. God is defiled. The host becomes terrified. And then, from out of nowhere someone bursts in, 'Don't be alarmed! Don't look so pale! There is someone in town named [insert your name here] who has the very spirit of God in them."
> Would anyone say that about you or me?
> Would they even think it?
> By the day to day way we live our lives, would they have any reason to?"
> (page 75)

4. What is holiness?

5. Scott Huot and GW Brazier began a website called Notproud.com, where people can post anonymous confessions. What confessions do you need to make? Who, besides God, do you need to ask for forgiveness from?

6. In what ways have you turned from the pleasures of Christ and chosen the wide, easy path of compromise and sin? Be specific?

7. What practical steps can you take in order to turn back toward the narrow path of God? Are there certain circumstances or situations that you could avoid?

Chapter 4: Materialism

1. In what ways are you like a raccoon? Are you currently in debt? Are you living above your means? Do you over prioritize money?

BURIED ALIVE: A DISCUSSION ON OVERCOMING THE "SEVEN LIFELESS SINS"

2. Do you and your family tithe consistently?

3. Do you agree with the following statement by John Stott? Why or why not?

> "John Stott once said our blindness to materialism is similar to the western culture's blindness to the sins of slavery in the eighteenth and nineteenth centuries. Today we look back in amazement that Christian people could not see it for the evil it was. And likely, thinks Stott, future generations, should they look back, will regard our day with the same perplexity: *How could they not have seen it?*" (page 95)

4. Did you realize before reading this chapter that 40,000 children die every day due to malnutrition? How do you feel about this reality? Even more importantly, what do you plan to do about it?

5. Where do we get our desires for larger, newer, and nicer things? Why do you and I place such a high value on fancy cars and snappy clothes? Are we being brainwashed by advertisers and retailers?

6. Does the notion of treating charity workers like celebrities seem odd? Why or why not? Describe a world where such is the norm:

7. In your own words, explain what this poem means:

"And I walked earth's highway, grieving,
In my rags and poverty,
Till I heard His voice inviting,
"Lift your hands to Me!"

So I turned my hands toward heaven,
And He filled them with a store
Of His own transcendent riches
Till they could contain no more.

And at last I comprehended
With my stupid mind and dull
That God could not pour His riches,
Into hands already full." (page 106)

Chapter 5: Busyness

1. Have you ever had the blessing of working with children or adults with disabilities? If so, describe your experience:

2. Have you ever found yourself living life with a "loss of direction"? What's the cause of your busyness in such times?

3. Did you find it difficult to formulate a mission statement of your own? In what ways was it beneficial to gather your thoughts and articulate your values?

4. If you were to make your own original list of "Ways to Enjoy Life" what would you write?

5. Do you have a consistent, daily quiet time? If so, where and when and how do you do it? If not, where and when and how could you?

6. What are some unimportant things that you often take too seriously?

7. What are some important things that you seldom take seriously enough?

Chapter 6: Laziness

1. Have you ever asked someone if they needed help, instead of just helping, in hopes that you wouldn't have to?

2. Have you ever asked God about something, when you already knew the answer, in hopes that you wouldn't have to do it?

3. If today were your last day on this earth how would you live it differently? What would you do? Where would you go? What would you say?

4. What are your thoughts on the following excerpt:

"Just the other day I read a bumper sticker that said: 'Working for God on earth doesn't pay much. But His

retirement plan is out of this world."...
I'm sure such a saying was not ill-intended, but I believe it is misinformed and misleading. In truth, the gospel is about *life*, not death. It is for *living*, not dying. And so if we simply await our "retirement plan" of eternal life then we are overlooking what God longs to do in our lives in the meantime. We are forfeiting the life we were intended." (page 151)

5. Take a few moments to really imagine it, then describe what you think it'd be like to meet God face to face and have Him tell you, "Well done, good and faithful servant!"

6. At those times when laziness has its tightest grip on your life what would you say is the reason?

7. Having read this chapter, how much of a threat do you feel laziness is on your life?
What practical ways do you plan to overcome it?

Chapter 7: Comfort

1. Like the woman who chooses her rose over her rose bearer, do you ever find yourself choosing personal comfort over the "God of all comfort"?

2. What are your thoughts on the list of "Scripture You Won't Likely Hear Preached on this Sunday at Church," starting on page 166?

3. In light of the previous list, and after having read this chapter, do you recognize times now in which you've dismissed or combated Scripture?

4. Do you believe the Bible to be literal? Why or why not?

5. Do you believe that there are contradictions in the Bible? Why or why not?

6. What are your thoughts on the following excerpt:

"After all, God certainly could have created a book devoid of contradiction if He wished. *But maybe there is something to be learned from the fact that He didn't.* Maybe there is some relevance to this idea of the Bible being a spiritual and relational thing after all!" (page 178)

7. What would you think if the second coming of Jesus Christ suddenly occurred?

Epilogue

1. What does life abundantly mean to you?

2. Even more importantly, how do you intend to achieve it?

3. Having completed the book and discussed each of the "Seven *Lifeless* Sins," which would you say you suffer from most?

4. Even more importantly, what do you intend to do about it?

5. Are you as ambitious as Shelby?

6. If you were to describe your life using only one adjective what word would you choose? Why?

7. If you were to add one sin to the list of "Seven *Lifeless* Sins" what would you add? Why?

Endnotes

Acknowledgments

[1] Donald Miller, *Searching for God Knows What* (Nashville, TN: Thomas Nelson Publishing, 2004), 128.

Introduction

[2] Deuteronomy 30:19
[3] John 10:10
[4] John 6:63
[5] 2 Corinthians 4:11
[6] John 1:4
[7] Colossians 2:13
[8] 1 Timothy 4:8
[9] Matthew 7:14
[10] 1 John 1:2
[11] Claire Folkard, ed. *Guinness Book of World Records 2005* (Guinness, 2004), 41.
[12] 1Timothy 6:19

Chapter 1: Tolerance

[13] 1 Thessalonians 3:8
[14] Acts 17:6
[15] 1 Timothy 2:5-6, John 14:6, John 10:16, Acts 4:12, 1 John 5:12
[16] 2 Timothy 3:16, Hebrews 4:12, John 1:1-4, Psalm 119:89, Matthew 24:35, 1 Peter 1:25, Ephesians 6:17
[17] Genesis 1:1, Psalm 19:1-6, Psalm 90:2, Jeremiah 51:15-16, Colossians 1:15-17, Hebrews 11:3
[18] Hebrews 13:4, Exodus 20:14, Proverbs 6:32, Matthew 5:27-28, Ezekiel 16:32
[19] Psalm 139:13-14, Isaiah 44:2, Ecclesiastes 11:5, Exodus 21:22-25
[20] Psalm 40:5, Romans 8:11, Daniel 3:22-27, Matthew 16:7-10, John 2:11, Ephesians 1:18-21
[21] "Beliefs: Salvation." The Barna Group. http://www.barna.org/FlexPage.aspx?Page=Topic&TopicID=4 (Nov 11, 2005).

[22] "Beliefs: Salvation." The Barna Group. http://www.barna.org/FlexPage.aspx?Page=Topic&TopicID=4 (Nov. 11, 2005).
[23] Patrick Morley, *Second Half of the Man in the Mirror* (Grand Rapids, MI: Zondervan Publishing, 1997), 118.
[24] Christianity Today. Jan. 2004. 19.
[25] "Mysteries of Faith." US News and World Report: Special Collector's Edition. 8.
[26] Revelation 3:16
[27] Judges 17:6
[28] John 18:38
[29] 2 Timothy 4:3
[30] Romans 14:1-22
[31] Ravi Zacharias, *Jesus Among Other Gods* (Nashville, TN: Word Publishing, 2000), 7.
[32] 1 Timothy 2:5-6
[33] 1 John 5:12
[34] John 14:6
[35] Acts 4:12
[36] Matthew 11:27
[37] John 10:16
[38] Luke 2:10
[39] John 3:17
[40] Proverbs 27:6
[41] "Mysteries of Faith." US News and World Report: Special Collector's Edition. 8.
[42] 2 Corinthians 5:17
[43] Matthew 4:17
[44] Anne R. Carey and Chad Palmer. "USA Today Snapshots." TNS Intersearch. (Feb. 20, 2004)
[45] Romans 14:13
[46] Luke 12:51, 54-57
[47] Acts 17:11
[48] Proverbs 16:21
[49] 1 Thessalonians 5:21-22
[50] 1 John 4:1-3
[51] Matthew 9:37
[52] Esther 4:14
[53] Leland H. Gregory, *What is the Number for 911?* (Kansas City, MO: Andrews McMeel Publishing, 2000).

[54] Matthew 10:22

Chapter 2: Fundamentalism

[55] Psalm 30:11
[56] John 5:8-11, John 4:7-9, John 8:1-7
[57] Colossians 2:20-21
[58] Ephesians 5:18
[59] Matthew 11:18-19, 1 Timothy 5:23
[60] Colossians 2:8
[61] Galatians 3:5
[62] Matthew 15:7-9
[63] Colossians 2:16-17
[64] Romans 10:4
[65] Psalm 149:3
[66] Mark 12:29-31
[67] Romans 13:9-10
[68] 1 Peter 4:8
[69] Galatians 5:14
[70] John 13:35
[71] Galatians 5:6
[72] 1 Corinthians 13:13
[73] 1Corinthians 13:1
[74] 1 Corinthians 13:3
[75] 1 Corinthians 13:2
[76] Ephesians 5:2
[77] 1 John 4:8
[78] 1 John 3:11
[79] 1 Corinthians 16:14
[80] 1 Timothy 1:5
[81] John 8:7
[82] John 8:11
[83] C. S. Lewis, "Footnote for a Prayer' in *The Pilgrim's Regress: An Allegorical Apology for Christianity Reason and Romanticism*, 144-45.
[84] Exodus 3:1-14
[85] Brian D. Mclaren and Tony Campolo, *Adventures in Missing the Point: How the Culture- Controlled Church Neutered the Gospel* (Grand Rapids, MI: Zondervan Publishing House, 2003), 32.
[86] 1 Corinthians 13:9-10, 12
[87] Titus 2:3-4, 1 Timothy 2:9-15, Galatians 3:28, Acts 18:26, Ephesians

2:13-22, Acts 2:17-18, Philippians 4:2-3, 1 Corinthians 14:34-35, 2 Corinthians 11:5, Romans 16:1-3, 6, 7, 12, 15, Ruth 4:11, Esther 9:12, Ezekiel 13:17, John 4:39, 1 Corinthians 11:3-16
[88] Genesis 19:5, Romans 1:24-27, Mark 10:6-9, Leviticus 18:22-23, Leviticus 20:13, Judges 19:22-24, 1 Corinthians 6:9-10, 1 Timothy 1:10
[89] Psalm 69:28, Hebrews 6:4-6, Matthew 12:31, Romans 8:38-39, Romans 11:11
[90] Genesis 1:1-3:24, 2 Peter 3:8, Hebrews 3:4, Psalm 19:1-6, Psalm 90:2, Jeremiah 51:15-16, Colossians 1:15-17, Hebrews 11:3, Genesis 4:16-17
[91] Matthew 5:31-32, Matthew 19:3-9, Mark 10:6-12, 1 Corinthians 7:10-15, 32-40, Malachi 2:13-16, Matthew 1:19,
[92] John 14:6, 1 Timothy 1:13, Romans 1:20, 2 Thessalonians 1:6-10, 1 Timothy 2:3-6, 1 John 5:12, Acts 4:2, John 10:16
[93] Genesis 11:1, Isaiah 36:11, Acts 19:1-7, 1 Corinthians 14:18, 1 Corinthians 14:39, 1 Corinthians 12:7-11, 1 Corinthians 12:28, 1 Corinthians 13:1, 1 Corinthians 14:2, 4- 5, 18, 22, 26-33
[94] Matthew 3:11, Mark 1:8, 1 Corinthians 1:17, 1 Peter 3:21, Mark 16:16, Acts 2:38, Romans 6:1-9, Matthew 28:18-20, Luke 22:7-20, 1 Corinthians 11:24-25, Romans 2:25-29, Romans 3:30, 1 Corinthians 7:19, Galatians 6:15, Titus 3:9, Colossians 2:8, 16-17, Galatians 3:5, Matthew 15:7-9, Romans 10:4
[95] Romans 8:29-30, Romans 9:10-21, Romans 11:25, Ephesians 1:4-5, 11, 2 Thessalonians 2:13, 2 Timothy 2:10, Psalm 33:12, Psalm 139:15-16, Isaiah 41:4, John 17:1-12, Acts 17:26, 1 Peter 2:8
[96] Luke 13:16, Matthew 4:1-11, Matthew 12:22, Mark 1:23-26, Mark 5:1-13, Mark 9:17-27, 1 Thessalonians 2:17-18, Luke 4:33-37, 2 Corinthians 2:11, 2 Corinthians 10:3-4, 2 Thessalonians 2:7-12, Ephesians 6:10-18, Hebrews 1:14, Hebrews 13:2, 1 John 4:2-3, 1 Peter 5:8, 2 Peter 2:11-12, Jude 1:9, James 4:7
[97] Proverbs 12:10, Genesis 1:26, Genesis 7:1-5, 23-24, Genesis 8:1,7, Luke 12:6, Luke 16:11-12, Exodus 23:12, Deuteronomy 22:4, Proverbs 30:25-28, Romans 1:20, Leviticus 25:2-8, Genesis 1:1, 10, 12, 18, 21, 25, 31, Genesis 1:26-28, Genesis 2:15, Exodus 9:29, Psalm 24:1, Psalm 19:1-6, Psalm 29:3, Psalm 33:5-7, Psalm 104:24, Psalm 136:1-9, Isaiah 6:3, Revelations 7:2-3, Revelations 9:4
[98] Galatians 2:10, 2 Corinthians 8:13-15, 2 Corinthians 9:7, Luke 16:1-13, 1 Timothy 6:6-11, 17-18, Malachi 3:5, 8-9, Psalms 62:10, James 5:1-6, Hebrews 13:5, Deuteronomy 8:11,17-18, Proverbs 3:9-10, Matthew 10:8, Matthew 13:22, Acts 20:35, Acts 5:1-11, James 1:9-10, Matthew 19:21, Mark 10:21, Luke 6:20, Luke 12:33-34, Luke 14:13-14, Luke 18:18-25,

Revelations 3:17

[99] Matthew 16:27, Matthew 19:28, Ephesians 6:8, Revelations 22:12, 1 Corinthians 3:12-15, 2 Corinthians 5:10, Matthew 5:11-12, Luke 6:23, 2 John 8

[100] Exodus 20:14, Romans 12:17-21, Romans 13:1-2, Romans 13:10, 1 Thessalonians 5:15,

[101] Genesis 18:20-33, Genesis 24:12-15, Mark 11:24, Exodus 16:3-5, 1 Samuel 12:18, 1 Samuel 15:10, 1 Samuel 28:5-19, 1 Kings 8:52, Psalm 6:9, Nehemiah 1:4, Job 22:12-14, Job 30:20, Psalm 34:17, Psalm 5:3, Psalm 55:17, Psalm 99:6, Psalm 109:4, Psalm 145:17-19, Proverbs 10:24, Isaiah 30:19, Isaiah 65:24

[102] Psalm 139: 13-14, Isaiah 44:2, Ecclesiastes 11:5, Exodus 21:22-25, Galatians 1:15

[103] John 1:1, 2 Timothy 3:16-17, Hebrews 4:12-13, Romans 10:8, Proverbs 30:5, Luke 4:4, Ephesians 6:17

[104] Genesis 12:1-3, Genesis 13:14-17, Genesis 32:28, Exodus 2:24, Exodus 3:10, Exodus 4:22, Exodus 5:1, Exodus 29:45, Exodus 32:13, Nehemiah 9:8, Psalm 105, Micah 7:2, Luke 1:68-75, Acts 14:4, Acts 17:12, Acts 18:6, Romans 1:16, Romans 2:28-29, Romans 3:9, 29, Romans 4, Romans 9:6, 30-31, Romans 10:11-12, 14, Romans 11:25-27, 1 Corinthians 12:13, Galatians 3:28, Hebrews 6:13-15, 8:10, Revelations 7:4

[105] Mark 13:1-37, Matthew 24:1-51, Luke 21:5-36, 1 Thessalonians 5:1-2, 2 Thessalonians 2:1-3, Ezekiel 38:17-39:16, 1 Peter 4:7, Matthew 28:20, 2 Peter 3:10

[106] 2 Timothy 3:12, Romans 8:28, 31-32, 1 Corinthians 4:11-13, 2 Corinthians 1:9, 2 Corinthians 11:23-28, 2 Corinthians 12:7-10, Philippians 1:12-14, 2 Timothy 1:11-12, Hebrews 12:6-11, James 1:2-4,12, 1 Peter 1:6-7, 1 John 3:13

[107] John 14:6, Romans 1:20, Romans 10:14-15, 2 Thessalonians 1:6-10, 1 Timothy 1:13, 1 Timothy 2:3-6, Titus 2:11, 1 John 5:12, Acts 4:2, John 10:16, Psalm 103:10, Ezekiel 33:11, Revelations 17:8, Revelations 20:7-15

[108] Mark 16:15 16

[109] Mark 16:17-18

[110] Romans 14:1-22

[111] 1 Corinthians 12:12-31

[112] Leviticus 25:2-8, Genesis 1:1, 10, 12, 18, 21, 25-28, 31, Genesis 2:15, Exodus 9:29, Psalm 24:1, Psalm 19:1-6, Psalm 29:3, Psalm 33:5-7, Psalm 104:24, Psalm 136:1-9, Isaiah 6:3, Revelations 7:2-3, Revelations 9:4,

Proverbs 12:10, Genesis 7:1-5, 23-24, Genesis 8:1,7, Luke 12:6, Exodus 23:12, Deuteronomy 22:4, Proverbs 30:25-28, Romans 1:20

[113] Titus 2:3-4, 1 Timothy 2:9-15, Galatians 3:28, Acts 18:26, Ephesians 2:13-22, Acts 2:17-18, Philippians 4:2-3, 1 Corinthians 14:34-35, 2 Corinthians 11:5, Romans 16:1-3, 6, 7, 12, 15

[114] Jim Wallis, *God's Politics* (New York, NY: HarperCollins Publishers Inc., 2005), back cover.

[115] 1 Thessalonians 5:18

[116] Titus 3:9

[117] 1 Corinthians 8:9, 1 Corinthians 6:12

Chapter 3: Compromise

[118] 2 Chronicles 7:14

[119] Tony Evans, *Are Christians Destroying America?* (Chicago, IL: Moody Press, 1996), 14, 15.

[120] "Family" The Barna Group. http://www.barna.org/FlexPage.aspx?Page=BarnaUpdate&BarnaUpdateID=170 (Nov. 11, 2005).

[121] Matthew 5:13

[122] Matthew 5:14

[123] 1 Peter 1:15

[124] 1 Thessalonians 4:7-8

[125] Ephesians 4:1

[126] Philippians 1:27

[127] 1 Timothy 5:22

[128] Romans 12:2

[129] Romans 12:9

[130] 1 Corinthians 3:17

[131] 1 Corinthians 6:19, 20

[132] 2 Corinthians 6:16, 17

[133] Hebrews 12:14

[134] Romans 7:24

[135] James Bryan Smith, *An Arrow Pointing to Heaven* (Nashville, TN: Broadman & Holman Publishing, 2000). 185.

[136] Frank E. Peretti, *The Oath* (Nashville, TN: WestBow Press, 2003). vii.

[137] Romans 7:18

[138] Romans 4:23

[139] Romans 3:10

[140] Scott Huot and GW Brazier, *Not Proud* (New York, NY: Simon Spotlight Entertainment, 2005).

[141] Leviticus 22:32
[142] Proverbs 28:13
[143] James 5:16
[144] Helen H Lemmel, Singspiration Music. 1922, 1950.
[145] Colossians 3:2
[146] 2 Timothy 2:22

Chapter 4: Materialism

[148] 1 Timothy 6:9-10
[149] "Credit Counseling Statistics: You are Not Along!" Credit Counseling Biz. http://www.creditcounselingbiz.com/credit_counseling statistics.htm (Feb. 2, 2005).
[150] Jamie H. Thompson. "Am I Trying to Shock You?" University of Missouri Outreach and Extension. http://outreach.missouri.edu/cmregion/thriving/archives2001/2001april/shock-you.html (April 4, 2005).
[151] http://www.fool.com/news/commentary/2004/commentary04093001.htm?logvisit=y&source=eptyholnk403200&bounce=y&bounce2=y (June 10, 2005).
[152] 1 Peter 2:16
[153] 1 Corinthians 7:23
[154] Erwin W. Lutzer, *Seven Snares of the Enemy* (Chicago, IL: Moody Press, 2001), 25.
[155] John 3:16
[156] "The Year's Most Intriguing Findings, From Barna Research Studies." The Barna Group. http://www.barna.org/FlexPage.aspx?Page=BarnaUpdate&BarnaUpdateID=103 (Nov. 10, 2005).
[157] Hebrews 13:5
[158] Matthew 19:24
[159] 1 John 3:17
[160] Luke 16:10-11
[161] Matthew 19:21
[162] 1 Timothy 6:10
[163] Proverbs 9:17
[164] Galatians 5:1
[165] R. Kent Hughes, *Set Apart: Calling A Worldly Church to A Godly Life* (Wheaton, IL: Crossway Books, 2003), 27.
[166] Brian D. Mclaren and Tony Campolo, *Adventures in Missing the Point: How the Culture-Controlled Church Neutered the Gospel* (Grand Rapids, MI: Zondervan Publishing House, 2003), 170.
[167] Brian D. Mclaren and Tony Campolo, *Adventures in Missing the Point: How the Culture-Controlled Church Neutered the Gospel* (Grand Rapids, MI:

Zondervan Publishing House, 2003), 62.
[168] 1 John 3:18
[169] 1 Corinthians 4:20
[170] James 2:15-17
[171] Tony Campolo, *20 Hot Potatoes Christians are Afraid to Touch* (W Publishing Group, 1988), 97.
[172] John 8:32
[173] Romans 8:1-2
[174] Romans 6:18
[175] John 8:36
[176] Matthew 10:29-31
[177] Philippians 4:11
[178] Philippians 4:12
[179] Proverbs 30:8-9
[180] 1 Timothy 6:6-7
[181] Luke 12:15
[182] 1 Timothy 6:3-5
[183] Ecclesiastes 3:11
[184] Philippians 3:20
[185] Psalm 119:19
[186] 1 Peter 2:11, 1 Peter 1:17
[187] John 17:16
[188] Ecclesiastes 5:10
[189] Martha Snell Nicholson, "Treasures," *Ivory Palaces* (Chicago: Moody Press, 1949).
[190] Matthew 6:24
[191] Matthew 6:33
[192] Psalm 37:4
[193] Isaiah 55:2
[194] Proverbs 11:28
[195] 1 Timothy 6:17-19
[196] Ecclesiastes 7:2
[197] James 4:14
[198] Hebrews 13:14
[199] Psalm 39:4
[200] 1 Corinthians 7:31
[201] Job 8:9
[202] 2 Corinthians 4:18
[203] 1 John 2:17
[204] Rick Warren, *Purpose Driven Life* (Grand Rapids, MI: Zondervan Publishing, 2002), 51.

Chapter 5: Busyness

[205] Luke 10:41,42
[206] "Self-Descriptions." The Barna Group. http://www.barna.org/FlexPage.aspx?Page=Topic&TopicID=34 (Nov. 1, 2005).
[207] "Personal Stress Solutions: About Stress." Stress Directions. http://www.stressdirections.com/personal/about_stress/index.html (Nov. 11, 2005).
[208] Deuteronomy 5:12
[209] Ephesians 5:17
[210] Ravi Zacharias, *Jesus Among Other Gods* (Nashville, TN: Word Publishing, 2000), 12.
[211] 1 Corinthians 9:26
[212] Psalm 37:23
[213] Proverbs 19:21
[214] Proverbs 16:3
[215] Ephesians 5:10
[216] Lewis Carroll, *Alice in Wonderland.*
[217] Emily Dickinson, "Not in Vain."
[218] Philippians 4:6
[219] Matthew 11:29-30
[220] Luke 12:25-26
[221] John 14:1
[222] Luke 12:27
[223] Proverbs 23:4
[224] Mark 1:35
[225] Matthew 13:14
[226] Luke 4:42
[227] Mark 6:31-32
[228] Kerby Anderson, "Time and Busyness." Probe Ministries. http://www.probe.org/content/view/908/72/ (Jan. 14, 2005).
[229] James C. Dobson, *Straight Talk to Men and Their Wives*

Chapter 6: Laziness

[230] Ephesians 4:16
[231] James 2:24
[232] Erwin Raphael McManus, *Seizing Your Divine Moment* (Nashville, TN: Thomas Nelson Publishers, 2002), 207.
[233] Ephesians 2:8, 9
[234] Ephesians 2:10

[235] James 2:26
[236] John 14:15
[237] Author unkown. Mark Water, ed. *The New Encyclopedia of Christian Quotations* (Grand Rapids, MI: Baker Books, 2000), 1129.
[238] Donald Miller, *Blue Like Jazz* (Nashville, TN: Thomas Nelson Publishers, 2003), 86.
[239] Ephesians 5:15, 16
[240] Dallas Willard, *The Divine Conspiracy* (New York, NY: Harper Collins Publishers, 1998), 12.
[241] Matthew 22:32
[242] Psalm 27:4
[243] 1 Peter 4:10
[244] 1 Timothy 4:14
[245] 1Corinthians 4:2
[246] Romans 6:13
[247] Ezekiel 33:4, 6
[248] Luke 12:48
[249] James 4:17
[250] Romans 1:18

Chapter 7: Comfort

[251] 1 Timothy 3:16
[252] 2 Corinthians 1:3
[253] Matthew 11:30
[254] "The Year's Most Intriguing Findings, From Barna Research Studies." The Barna Group. http://www.barna.org?FlexPage.aspx?Page=BarnaUpdate&BarnaUpdateID=77 (Nov. 6, 2005).
[255] "Americans Identify What They Want Out of Life." The Barna Group. http://www.barna.org/FlexPage.aspx?Page=BarnaUpdate&BarnaUpdateID=57 (Nov. 6, 2005).
[256] C. S. Lewis, *Miracles*.
[257] Ecclesiastes 1:14
[258] Hosea 9:15
[259] Romans 9:13
[260] Mark 3:29
[261] Matthew 12:31
[262] 1 Corinthians 11:7, 6
[263] 1 Corinthians 15:29
[264] 1 Samuel 15:3

[265] Ezekiel 9:5, 6
[266] Deuteronomy 23:1-2 (RSV)
[267] Genesis 38:9-10
[268] Leviticus 26:27, 29
[269] Luke 10:25-28
[270] 1 Timothy 2:14-15
[271] Psalm 42:7, Romans 8:26
[272] John 1:29
[273] 1 Peter 5:8
[274] Luke 3:16
[275] Genesis 1:25-26, Genesis 2:18-19
[276] 1 Kings 4:26, 2 Chronicles 9:25
[277] 2 Samuel 24:13, 1 Chronicles 21:11
[278] 1 Samuel 31:4-6, 2 Samuel 1:15
[279] Luke 4:5-9, Matthew 4:5-8
[280] Mark 6:8, Luke 9:3, Matthew 10:9-10
[281] Matthew 21:12, Mark 11:11-16
[282] Matthew 17:1, Mark 9:2, Luke 9:28-29
[283] Matthew 27:34, Mark 15:23
[284] Matthew 28:1, Mark 16:1, John 20:1
[285] Matthew 28:2-5, Mark 16:5, Luke 24:4, John 20:12
[286] Matthew 28:8, Luke 24:9, John 20:18, Mark 16:8
[287] Matthew 27:5, Acts 1:18
[288] John 5:39-40
[289] A. W. Tozer, *The Knowledge of the Holy* (Lincoln, Nebraska: Back to the Bible Broadcast, 1976), 9, 10.
[290] 1 Corinthians 13:11
[291] Hebrews 5:12
[292] Hebrews 6:1
[293] Ephesians 4:14
[294] 1 Corinthians 14:20
[295] Donald Miller, *Blue Like Jazz* (Nashville, TN: Thomas Nelson Publishers, 2003), 205, 206.
[296] Titus 2:3-4, 1 Timothy 2:9-15, Galatians 3:28, Acts 18:26, Ephesians 2:13-22, Acts 2:17-18, Philippians 4:2-3, 1 Corinthians 14:34-35, 2 Corinthians 11:5, Romans 16:1-3, 6, 7, 12, 15, Ruth 4:11, Esther 9:12, Ezekiel 13:17, John 4:39, 1 Corinthians 11:3-16
[297] Genesis 19:5, Romans 1:24-27, Mark 10:6-9, Leviticus 18:22-23, Leviticus 20:13, Judges 19:22-24, 1 Corinthians 6:9-10, 1 Timothy 1:10
[298] Psalm 69:28, Hebrews 6:4-6, Matthew 12:31, Romans 8:38-39, Romans 11:11
[299] Genesis 1:1-3:24, 2 Peter 3:8, Hebrews 3:4, Psalm 19:1-6, Psalm 90:2,

Jeremiah 51:15-16, Colossians 1:15-17, Hebrews 11:3, Genesis 4:16-17

[300] Matthew 5:31-32, Matthew 19:3-9, Mark 10:6-12, 1 Corinthians 7:10-15, 32-40, Malachi 2:13-16, Matthew 1:19

[301] John 14:6, 1 Timothy 1:13, Romans 1:20, 2 Thessalonians 1:6-10, 1 Timothy 2:3-6, 1 John 5:12, Acts 4:2, John 10:16

[302] Genesis 11:1, Isaiah 36:11, Acts 19:1-7, 1 Corinthians 12:7-11, 28, 1 Corinthians 13:1, 1 Corinthians 14:2, 4-5, 18, 22, 26-33, 39

[303] Matthew 3:11, Mark 1:8, 1 Corinthians 1:17, 1 Peter 3:21, Mark 16:16, Acts 2:38, Romans 6:1-9, Matthew 28:18-20, Luke 22:7-20, 1 Corinthians 11:24-25, Romans 2:25-29, Romans 3:30, 1 Corinthians 7:19, Galatians 6:15, Titus 3:9, Colossians 2:8, 16-17, Galatians 3:5, Matthew 15:7-9, Romans 10:4

[304] Romans 8:29-30, Romans 9:10-21, Romans 11:25, Ephesians 1:4-5,11, 2 Thessalonians 2:13, 2 Timothy 2:10, Psalm 33:12, Psalm 139:15-16, Isaiah 41:4, John 17:1-12, Acts 17:26, 1 Peter 2:8

[305] Luke 13:16, Matthew 4:1-11, Matthew 12:22, Mark 1:23-26, Mark 5:1-13, Mark 9:17-27, 1 Thessalonians 2:17-18, Luke 4:33-37, 2 Corinthians 2:11, 2 Corinthians 10:3-4, 2 Thessalonians 2:7-12, Ephesians 6:10-18, Hebrews 1:14, Hebrews 13:2, 1 John 4:2-3, 1 Peter 5:8, 2 Peter 2:11-12, Jude 1:9, James 4:7

[306] Proverbs 12:10, Genesis 1:26, Genesis 7:1-5, 23-24, Genesis 8:1,7, Luke 12:6, Exodus 23:12, Deuteronomy 22:4, Proverbs 30:25-28, Romans 1:20

[307] Leviticus 25:2-8, Genesis 1:1, 10, 12, 18, 21, 25, 26-28, 31, Genesis 2:15, Exodus 9:29, Psalm 24:1, Psalm 19:1-6, Psalm 29:3, Psalm 33:5-7, Psalm 104:24, Psalm 136:1-9, Isaiah 6:3, Revelations 7:2-3, Revelations 9:4

[308] Galatians 2:10, 2 Corinthians 8:13-15, 2 Corinthians 9:7, Luke 16:1-13, 1 Timothy 6:6-11, 17-18, Malachi 3:5, 8-9, Psalms 62:10, James 5:1-6, Hebrews 13:5, Deuteronomy 8:11, 17-18, Proverbs 3:9-10, Matthew 10:8, Matthew 13:22, Acts 20:35, Acts 5:1-11, James 1:9-10, Matthew 19:21, Mark 10:21, Luke 6:20, Luke 12:33-34, Luke 14:13-14, Luke 18:18-25, Revelations 3:17

[309] Matthew 16:27, Matthew 19:28, Ephesians 6:8, Revelations 22:12, 1 Corinthians 3:12-15, 2 Corinthians 5:10, Matthew 5:11-12, Luke 6:23, 2 John 8

[310] Exodus 20:14, Romans 12:17-21, Romans 13:1-2, Romans 13:10, 1 Thessalonians 5:15,

[311] Genesis 18:20-33, Genesis 24:12-15, Mark 11:24, Exodus 16:3-5, 1 Samuel 12:18, 1 Samuel 15:10, 1 Samuel 28:5-19, 1 Kings 8:52, Psalm 6:9, Nehemiah 1:4, Job 22:12-14, Job 30:20, Psalm 34:17, Psalm 5:3, Psalm 55:17, Psalm 99:6, Psalm 109:4, Psalm 145:17-19, Proverbs 10:24,

Isaiah 30:19, Isaiah 65:24

[312] Psalm 139: 13-14, Isaiah 44:2, Ecclesiastes 11:5, Exodus 21:22-25, Galatians 1:15

[313] Psalm 139: 13-14, Isaiah 44:2, Ecclesiastes 11:5, Exodus 21:22-25, Galatians 1:15

[314] John 1:1, 2 Timothy 3:16-17, Hebrews 4:12-13, Romans 10:8, Proverbs 30:5, Luke 4:4, Ephesians 6:17

[315] Genesis 12:1-3, Genesis 13:14-17, Genesis 32:28, Exodus 2:24, Exodus 3:10, Exodus 4:22, Exodus 5:1, Exodus 29:45, Exodus 32:13, Nehemiah 9:8, Psalm 105, Micah 7:2, Luke 1:68-75, Acts 14:4, Acts 17:12, Acts 18:6, Romans 1:16, Romans 2:28-29, Romans 3:9, 29, Romans 4, Romans 9:6, 30-31, Romans 10:11-14, Romans 11:25-27, 1 Corinthians 12:13, Galatians 3:28, Hebrews 6:13-15, Hebrews 8:10, Revelations 7:4

[316] Mark 13:1-37, Matthew 24:1-51, Luke 21:5-36, 1 Thessalonians 5:1-2, 2 Thessalonians 2:1-3, Ezekiel 38:17-39:16, 1 Peter 4:7, Matthew 28:20, 2 Peter 3:10

[317] 2 Timothy 3:12, Romans 8:28, Romans 8:31-32, 1 Corinthians 4:11-13, 2 Corinthians 1:9, 2 Corinthians 11:23-28, 2 Corinthians 12:7-10, Philippians 1:12-14, 2 Timothy 1:11-12, Hebrews 12:6-11, James 1:2-4,12, 1 Peter 1:6-7, 1 John 3:13

[318] John 14:6, Romans 1:20, Romans 10:14-15, 2 Thessalonians 1:6-10, 1 Timothy 1:13, 1 Timothy 2:3-6, Titus 2:11, 1 John 5:12, Acts 4:2, John 10:16, Psalm 103:10, Ezekiel 33:11, Revelations 17:8, Revelations 20:7-15

Epilogue

[319] Matthew 7:7

For more information and availability about booking Jenkins to speak before your congregation, group or organization, please send your inquiries to the following address: jenkinsbookinginfo@yahoo.com
Or call: (501) 860-8816.